Charles Kingsley

The King of the earth

and other sermons on national subjects, preached in a village church

Charles Kingsley

The King of the earth
and other sermons on national subjects, preached in a village church

ISBN/EAN: 9783744744713

Printed in Europe, USA, Canada, Australia, Japan

Cover: Foto ©Lupo / pixelio.de

More available books at **www.hansebooks.com**

THE KING OF THE EARTH

*AND OTHER
SERMONS ON NATIONAL SUBJECTS*

PREACHED IN A VILLAGE CHURCH

BY

CHARLES KINGSLEY

RECTOR OF EVERSLEY AND CANON OF CHESTER

SECOND EDITION

London:
MACMILLAN AND CO.
1872.

CONTENTS.

SERMON I. (p. 1.)
THE KING OF THE EARTH.
Behold, thy King cometh unto thee.—MATTHEW xxi. 4.

SERMON II. (p. 12.)
HOLY SCRIPTURE.
Whatsoever things were written aforetime, were written for our example, that we, through patience, and comfort of the Scriptures, might have hope.—ROMANS xv. 4.

SERMON III. (p. 22.)
THE KINGDOM OF GOD.
Now when John had heard in the prison the works of Christ, he sent two of his disciples, and said unto him, Art thou he that should come, or do we look for another? Jesus answered and said unto them, Go and show John again those things which ye do see and hear: The blind receive their sight, and the lame walk, the lepers are cleansed, and the deaf hear, the dead are raised up, and the poor have the gospel preached to them.—MATTHEW xi. 2, 3, 4, 5.

SERMON IV. (p. 40.)
A PREPARATION FOR CHRISTMAS.
Rejoice in the Lord always.—PHILIPPIANS iv. 4.

SERMON V. (p. 50.)
CHRISTMAS DAY.
He made himself of no reputation, and took upon him the form of a slave.—PHILIPPIANS ii. 7.

SERMON VI. (p. 60.)
TRUE ABSTINENCE.
I keep under my body, and bring it into subjection.—1 CORINTHIANS ix. 27.

CONTENTS.

SERMON VII. (p. 76.)
GOOD FRIDAY.

In all their affliction He was afflicted, and the angel of His presence saved them. In His love and in His pity He redeemed them; and He bare them and carried them all the days of old.—ISAIAH lxiii. 9.

SERMON VIII. (p. 87.)
EASTER-DAY.

If ye then be risen with Christ, seek those things which are above, where Christ sitteth on the right hand of God.—COLOSSIANS iii. 1.

SERMON IX. (p. 99.)
THE COMFORTER.

If I go not away, the Comforter will not come unto you; but if I depart, I will send Him unto you.—JOHN xvi. 7.

SERMON X. (p. 111.)
WHIT-SUNDAY.

The fruit of the Spirit is love, joy, peace, longsuffering, gentleness, goodness, faith, meekness, temperance—against such there is no law.—GALATIANS v. 22, 23.

SERMON XI. (p. 130.)
ASCENSION-DAY.

And Jesus led them out as far as to Bethany; and he lifted up his hands and blessed them. And it came to pass while he blessed them, he was parted from them, and carried up into heaven. And they worshipped him and returned to Jerusalem, with great joy; and were continually in the temple, praising and blessing God.—LUKE xxiv. 50—53

SERMON XII. (p. 142.)
THE FOUNT OF SCIENCE.

When He ascended up on high, He led captivity captive, and received gifts for men, yea, even for his enemies, that the Lord God might dwell among them.—PSALM lxviii. 18, and EPHESIANS iv. 8.

CONTENTS. vii

SERMON XIII. (p. 177.)
FIRST SERMON ON THE CHOLERA.
God's judgments are from above, out of the sight of the wicked.—PSALM x. 5.

SERMON XIV. (p. 190.)
SECOND SERMON ON THE CHOLERA.
Visiting the sins of the fathers upon the children.—EXODUS xx. 5.

SERMON XV. (p. 203.)
THIRD SERMON ON THE CHOLERA.
I the Lord thy God am a jealous God, visiting the iniquity of the fathers upon the children, unto the third and fourth generation of them that hate me.—EXODUS xx. 5.

SERMON XVI. (p. 217.)
ON THE DAY OF THANKSGIVING.
God hath visited his people.—LUKE vii. 16.

SERMON XVII. (p. 231.)
THE COVENANT.
The Lord hath chosen Jacob unto himself, and Israel for his own possession. For I know that the Lord is great, and that our Lord is above all gods. Whatsoever the Lord pleased, that did he in heaven and earth, and in the sea, and in all deep places.—PSALM cxxxv. 4, 5, 6.

SERMON XVIII. (p. 244.)
NATIONAL REWARDS AND PUNISHMENTS.
And that which cometh into your mind shall not be at all; that ye say, We will be as the heathen, as the families of the countries, to serve wood and stone. As I live, saith the Lord God, surely with a mighty hand, and with a stretched out arm, and with fury poured out, will I rule over you. . . . . And ye shall know that I am the Lord.—EZEKIEL xx. 32, 33, 38.

CONTENTS.

SERMON XIX. (p. 254.)
THE DELIVERANCE OF JERUSALEM.

And it came to pass that night, that the angel of the Lord went out, and smote in the camp of the Assyrians an hundred and eighty-five thousand; and when they arose in the morning, behold, they were all dead corpses.—2 KINGS xix. 35.

SERMON XX. (p. 265.)
PROFESSION AND PRACTICE.

Though they say, 'The Lord liveth,' surely they swear falsely. —JEREMIAH V. 2.

SERMON XXI. (p. 279.)
THE UNFAITHFUL SERVANT.

But and if that servant say in his heart, My Lord delayeth His coming; and shall begin to beat the men servants and the maid servants, and to eat and drink and to be drunken; the Lord of that servant will come in a day when he looketh not for Him, and in an hour when he is not aware, and will cut him asunder, and will appoint him his portion with the unbelievers—LUKE xii. 45, 46.

SERMON XXII. (p. 294.)
THE WAY TO WEALTH.

Seek ye the Lord while He may be found, call ye upon Him while He is near: Let the wicked forsake his way, and the unrighteous man his thoughts: and let him return unto the Lord, and He will have mercy upon him, and to our God, for He will abundantly pardon.—ISAIAH lv. 6, 7.

SERMON XXIII. (p. 305.)
THE LOVE OF CHRIST.

For the love of Christ constraineth us; because we thus judge, that if one died for all, then were all dead. And that He died for all, that they which live should not henceforth live unto themselves, but unto Him which died for them, and rose again. —2 CORINTHIANS V. 14, 15.

I.

THE KING OF THE EARTH.

FIRST SUNDAY IN ADVENT.

MATTHEW xxi. 4.

Behold, thy King cometh unto thee.

[Preached in 1849.]

THIS Sunday is the first of the four Sundays in Advent. During those four Sundays, our forefathers have advised us to think seriously of the coming of our Lord Jesus Christ—not that we should neglect to think of it at all times. As some of you know, I have preached to you about it often lately. Perhaps before the end of Advent, you will all of you, more or less, understand what all that I have said about the cholera, and public distress, and the sins of this nation, and the sins of the labouring people, has to do with the coming of our Lord Jesus Christ. But I intend, especially in my next four sermons, to speak my whole mind to you about this matter as far as God has shown it to me; taking the Collect, Epistle, and Gospels, for each

Sunday in Advent, and explaining them. I am sure I cannot do better; for the more I see of those Collects, Epistles, and Gospels, and the way in which they are arranged, the more I am astonished and delighted at the wisdom with which they are chosen, the wise order in which they follow each other, and fit into each other. It is very fit, too, that we should think of our Lord's coming at this season of the year above all others; because it is the hardest season—the season of most want, and misery, and discontent, when wages are low, and work is scarce, and fuel is dear, and frosts are bitter, and farmers and tradesmen, and gentlemen, too, are at their wits' end to square their accounts, and pay their way. Then is the time that the evils of society come home to us— that our sins, and our sorrows, which, after all, are the punishment of our sins, stare us in the face. Then is the time, if ever, for men's hearts to cry out for a Saviour, who will deliver them out of their miseries and their sins; for a Heavenly King who will rule them in righteousness, and do justice and judgment on the earth, and see that those who are in need and necessity have right; for a Heavenly Counsellor who will guide them into all truth—who will teach them what they are, and whither they are going, and what the Lord requires of them. I say the hard days of winter are a fit time to turn men's hearts to Christ their King—the fittest of all times for a clergyman to get up in his pulpit, as I do now, and tell his people, as I tell you, that Jesus Christ your King has not forgotten you—that he is coming speedily to judge the world, and execute justice and judgment for the meek of the earth.

Now do not be in a hurry, and fancy from what I have just said, that I am one of those who think the end of the world is at hand. It may be, for aught I know. 'Of that day and that hour knoweth no man, not even the angels of God, nor the Son, but the Father only.' If you wish for my own opinion, I believe that what people commonly call the end of the world, that is, the end of the earth and of mankind on it, is not at hand at all. As far as I can judge from Scripture, and from the history of all nations, the earth is yet young, and mankind in its infancy. Five thousand years hence, our descendants may be looking back on us as foolish barbarians, in comparison with what they know: just as we look back upon the ignorance of people a thousand years ago. And yet I believe that the end of this world, in the real Scripture sense of the word 'world,' is coming very quickly and very truly—The end of this system of society, of these present ways in religion, and money-making, and conducting ourselves in all the affairs of life, which we English people have got into now-a-days. The end of it is coming. It cannot last much longer; for it is destroying itself. It will not last much longer; for Christ and not the devil is the King of the earth. As St. Paul said to his people, so say I to you, 'The night is far spent, the day is at hand.'

These may seem strange words, but almost every one is saying them, in his own way. One large party among religious people in these days is complaining that Christ has left His Church, and that the cause of Christianity will be ruined and lost, unless some great change takes place. Another large party of religious people say, that the prophecies are on the point of being all fulfilled; that the 1260 days, spoken of by the prophet Daniel, are just coming to an end; and that Christ is coming with His saints, to reign openly upon earth for a thousand years. The wisest philosophers and historians of late years have been all foretelling a great and tremendous change in England, and throughout all Europe; and in the mean time, manufacturers and landlords, tradesmen and farmers, artisans and labourers, all say, that there *must* be a change and will be a change. I believe they are all right, every one of them. They put it in their words; I think it better to put it in the Scripture words, and say boldly, 'Jesus Christ, the King of the earth, is coming.'

But you will ask, 'What right have you to stand up and say anything so surprising?' My friends, the world is full of surprising things, and this age above all ages. It was not sixty years ago, that a nobleman was laughed at in the House of Lords, for saying that he believed that we should one day see ships go by steam; and now there are steamers on every sea and ocean in the world. Who expected twenty years ago to see the whole face of England covered with these wonderful railroads? Who expected on the 22nd of February last year, that, within a single month, half the nations of Europe, which looked so quiet and secure, would be shaken from top to bottom with revolution and bloodshed—kings and princes vanishing one after the other like a dream—poor men sitting for a day as rulers of kingdoms, and then hurled down again to make room for other rulers as unexpected as themselves? Can any one consider the last fifty years?—can any one consider that one last year, 1848, and then not feel that we do live in a most strange and awful time? a time for which nothing is too surprising—a time in which we all ought to be prepared, from the least to the greatest, to see the greatest horrors and the greatest blessings come suddenly upon us, like a thief in the night? So much for Christ's coming being too wonderful a thing to happen just now. Still you are right to ask, 'What do you mean by Christ's being our King? what do you mean by His coming to us? What reason have you for supposing that He is coming *now*, rather than at any other time? And if He be coming, what are we to do? What is there we ought to repent of? what is there we ought to amend?

Well, my friends—it is just these very questions which I hope and trust God will help me to answer to you, in my next few sermons—I am perfectly convinced that we must get them answered and act upon them speedily. I am perfectly convinced that if we go on as most of us are going in England now, the Lord of us all will come in an hour when we are not aware, and cut us asunder in the deepest and most real sense, as He came and cut asunder France, Germany, and Austria only last year, and appoint us our portion with the unbelievers. And I believe that our punishment will be seven times as severe as that of either France, Germany, or Austria, because we have had seven times their privileges and blessings, seven times their Gospel light and Christian knowledge, seven times their freedom and justice in laws and constitution; seven times their wealth, and prosperity, and means of employing our population.

Much has been given to England, and of her much will be required. And if you could only see the state of mankind over the greatest part of the globe, how infinitely fewer opportunities they have of knowing God's will than you have, you would feel that to you, poor and struggling as some of you are—to you much has been given, and of you much will be required.

Now first, what do I mean by Christ being our king? I dare say there are some among you who are inclined to think that, when we talk of Christ being a king, that the word king means something very different from its common meaning—and, God knows, that that is true enough. Our blessed Lord took care to make people understand that —how He was not like one of the kings of the nations, how His kingdom was not of this world. But yet the Bible tells us again and again that all good kings, all real kings, are patterns of Christ; and, therefore, that when we talk of Christ being a king, we mean that He is a king in everything that a king ought to be; that He fulfils perfectly all the duties of a king; that He is the pattern which all kings ought to copy. Kings have been in all ages too apt to forget that, and, indeed, so have the people too. We English have forgotten most thoroughly in these days, that Christ is our king, or even a king at all. We talk of Christ being a 'spiritual' king, and then we say that that merely means that He is king of Christians' hearts. And when any one asks what that means, it comes out, that all we mean is, that Christ has a very great influence over the hearts of believing Christians—when He can obtain it; or else that it means that He is king of a very small number of people called the elect, whom He has chosen out, but that He has absolutely nothing to do with the whole rest of the world. And then, when any one stands up with the Bible in his hand, and says, in the plain words of Scripture, 'Christ is not only the king of believers, He is the king of the whole earth; the king of the clouds and the thunder, the king of the land and the cattle, and the trees, and the corn, and to whomsoever He will He giveth them. Christ is not only the king of believers—He is the king of all—the king of the wicked, of the heathen, of those who do not believe Him, who never heard of Him. Christ is not only the king of a few individual persons, one here and one there in every parish, but He is the king of every nation. He is the king of England, by the grace of God, just as much as Queen Victoria is, and ten thousand times more.'—If any man talks in this way, people stare—think him an enthusiast—ask him what new doctrine this is, and call his words unscriptural, just because they come out of Scripture and not out of men's perversions and twistings of Scripture. Nevertheless Christ is King; really and truly King of Kings and Lord of Lords; and He will make men know it. What He was, that He is and ever will be; there is no change in Him; His kingdom is an everlasting kingdom, and His dominion endureth throughout all ages, and woe unto those, small or great, who rebel against Him!

But what sort of a king is He? He is a king of law, and order, and justice. He is not selfish, fanciful, self-willed. He said himself that He came not to do His own will, but His Father's. He is a king of gentleness and meekness too : but do not mistake that. There is no weak indulgence in Him. A man may be very meek, and yet stern enough and strong enough. Moses was the meekest of men, we read, and yet He made those who rebelled against him feel that he was not to be trifled with. Korah, Dathan, and Abiram found that to their cost. He would not even spare his own brother Aaron, his own sister Miriam, when they rebelled. And he was right. He showed his love by it; indulgence is not love. It is no sign of meekness, but only of cowardice and carelessness, to be afraid to rebuke sin. Moses knew that he was doing God's work, that he was appointed to make a great nation of those slavish besotted Jews, his countrymen; that he was sent by God with boundless blessings to them; and woe to whoever hindered him from that. Because he loved the Jews, therefore he dared punish those who tempted them to forget the promised land of Canaan, or break God's covenant, in which lay all their hope.

And such a one is our King, my friends; Jesus Christ the Son of God. Like Moses, says St. Paul, He is faithful in all His office. Therefore He is severe as well as gentle. He was so when on earth. With the poor, the outcast, the neglected, those on whom men trampled, who was gentler than the Lord Jesus? To the proud Pharisee, the canting Scribe, the cunning Herodian, who was sterner than the Lord Jesus? Read that awful 23rd chapter of St. Matthew, and then see how the Saviour, the lamb dumb before his shearers, He of whom it was said 'He shall not strive nor cry, nor shall his voice be heard in the streets'—how he could speak when he had occasion. . . . 'Woe unto you Scribes and Pharisees, hypocrites!' 'Ye serpents, ye generation of vipers, how can ye escape the damnation of hell?'

My friends, those were the words of our King; of Him in whom was neither passion nor selfishness; who loved us even to the death, and endured for us the scourge, the cross, the grave. And believe me, such are His words now; though we do not hear Him, the heaven and the earth hear Him and obey Him. His message is pardon, mercy, deliverance, to the sorrowful and the oppressed, and the neglected; and to the proud, the tyrannical, the self-righteous, the hypocritical, tribulation, and anguish, shame and woe.

Because He is the Saviour, therefore He is a consuming fire to all those who try to hinder Him from saving men. Because He is the Son of God, He will sweep out of his Father's kingdom all who offend, and whosoever maketh and loveth a lie. Because He is boundless mercy and love, therefore He will show no mercy to those who try to stop his purposes of love. Because He is the King of men, the enemies of mankind are his enemies; and He will reign till He has put them all under his feet.

II.

HOLY SCRIPTURE.

SECOND SUNDAY IN ADVENT.

ROMANS XV. 4.

Whatsoever things were written aforetime, were written for our example, that we, through patience and comfort of the Scriptures, might have hope.

1. 'WHATSOEVER was written aforetime.'— There is no doubt, I think, that by these words St. Paul means the Bible; that is, the Old Testament, which was the only part of the Bible already written in his time. For it is of the Psalms which he is speaking. He mentions a verse out of the 69th Psalm, 'The reproaches of Him that reproached thee fell on me;' which, he says, applies to Christ just as much as it did to David, who wrote it. Christ, he says, pleased not himself any more than David, but suffered willingly and joyfully for God's sake, because he knew that he was doing God's work. And we, he goes on to say, must do the same; do as Christ did; we must not please our-

selves, but every one of us please our brother for his good and edification; that is, in order to build him up, strengthen him, make him wiser, better, more comfortable. For, he says, Christ pleased not himself, but like David, lived only to help others; and therefore this verse out of David's Psalms, 'The reproaches of them that reproached thee fell on me,' is a lesson to us; a pattern of what we ought to feel, and do, and suffer. 'For whatsoever was written aforetime,' all these ancient psalms and prophets, and histories of men and nations who trusted in God, 'were written for our example, that we, through patience and comfort of the Scriptures, might have hope.'

Yes, my friends, this is true; and the longer you live a life of faith and godliness, the longer you read and study that precious Book of books which God has put so freely into your hands in these days, the more true you will find it. And if it was true of the Old Testament, written before The Lord came down and dwelt among men, how much more must it be true of the New Testament, which was written after His coming by apostles and evangelists, who had far fuller light and knowledge of the Lord than ever David or the old prophets, even in their happiest moments, had. Ah, what a treasure you have, every one of you, in those Bibles of yours, which too many of you read so little! From the first chapter of Genesis to the last of Revelations, it is all written for our example, all profitable for teaching, for reproof, for correction, for instruction in righteousness, that the man of God may be perfect, thoroughly furnished for all good works. Ah! friends, friends, is not this the reason why so many of you do not read your Bibles, that you do not wish to be furnished for good works?—do not wish to be men of God, godly and godlike men, but only to be men of the world, caring only for money and pleasure?—some of you, alas! not wishing to be men and women at all, but only a sort of brute beasts with clothes on, given up to filth and folly, like the animals that perish, or rather worse than the animals, for they could be no better if they tried, but you might be. Oh! what might you not be, what are you not already, if you but knew it! Members of Christ, children of God, heirs of the kingdom of heaven, heirs of a hope undying, pure, that will never fade away, having a right given you by the promise and oath of Almighty God himself, to hope for yourselves, for your neighbours, for this poor distracted world, for ever and ever; a right to believe that there is an everlasting day of justice, and peace, and happiness in store for the whole world, and that you, if you will, may have your share in that glorious sunrise which shall never set again. You may have your share in it, each and every one of you; and if you ask why, go to the Scriptures, and there read the promises of God, the grounds of your just hope, for all heaven and earth.

First, of hope for yourselves.—I say first for yourselves, not because a man is right in being selfish, and caring only for his own soul, but because a man must care for his own soul first, if he ever intends to care for others; a man must have hope for himself first, if he is to have hope for others. He may stop there, and turn his religion into a selfish superstition, and spend his life in asking all day long, 'Shall I be saved, shall I be damned?' or worse still, in chuckling over his own good fortune, and saying to himself, 'I shall be saved, whoever else is damned;' but whether he ends there or not, he must begin there; begin by trying to get himself saved. For if he does not know what is right and good for himself, how can he tell what is right and good for others? If he wishes to bring his neighbours out of their sins, he must surely first have been brought out of his own sins, and so know what forgiveness and sanctification means. If he wishes to make others at peace with God, he must first be at peace with God himself, to know what God's peace is. If he wants to teach others their duty, he must first know his own duty, for all men's duty is one and the same. If he wishes to have hope for the world, he must first have hope for himself, for he is in the world, a part of it, and he must learn what blessings God intends for him, and they will teach him what blessings God has in store for the earth. Faith and hope, like charity, must begin at home. By learning the corruption of our own hearts, we learn the corruption of human nature. By learning what is the only medicine which can cure our own sick hearts, we learn what is the only medicine which can cure human nature. We learn by our own experience, that God is all-forgiving love; that his peace shines bright upon the soul which casts itself utterly on Jesus Christ the Lord for pardon, strength, and safety; that God's spirit is ready and able to raise us out of all our sin, and sottishness, and weakness, and wilfulness, and selfishness, and renew us into quite new men, different characters from what we used to be; and so, by having hope for ourselves, we learn step by step and year by year to have hope for our friends, for our neighbours, and for the whole world.

For that is another great lesson which the Bible teaches us—hope for the world. Men say to us, 'This world has always gone on ill, and will always go on so. Tyrants and knaves and hypocrites have always had the power in it; idlers have always had the enjoyment of it; while the humble, and industrious, and godly, who would not foul their hands with the wicked ways of the world, have been always laughed at, neglected, oppressed, persecuted. The world,' they say, 'is very bad, and we cannot live in it without giving way a little to its badness, and going the old road.'

But he who, through patience and comfort of the Scriptures, has hope, can answer 'Yes—and yet no.' 'Yes—we agree that the world has gone on badly enough: perhaps we think the world worse than it thinks itself; for God's Spirit has taught us to see sin, and shame, and ruin, in many a thing which the world thinks right and reasonable. And yet,' says the true Christian man, ' although we think the world worse than any one else thinks it, and are more unhappy than any one else about all the sin, and injustice, and misery we see in it, we have the very strongest faith—we are perfectly certain—we are as sure as if we saw it coming to pass here before us, that the world will come right at last. For the Bible tells us that the Son of God is the king of the world; that He has been the master and ruler of it from the beginning. He, the Bible tells us, condescended to come down on earth and be born in the likeness of a poor man, and die on the cross for this poor world of

His, that He might take away the sins of it.' 'Behold the Lamb of God,' said John the Baptist, 'who takes away the sin of the world.' How dare we, who call ourselves Christians, we who have been baptized into His name, we who have tasted of His mercy, we who know the might of His love, the converting and renewing power of His Spirit—how dare we doubt but that He *will* take away the sins of the world? Ay; step by step, nation by nation, year by year, the Lord shall conquer; love and justice, and wisdom shall spread and grow; for He must reign till He has put all enemies under His feet. He has promised to take away the sins of the world, and He is God, and cannot lie. There is the Christian's hope: let him leave infidels to say 'The world always was bad, and it must remain so to the end;' the Christian ought to be able to answer, 'The world was bad, and is bad; but for that very reason it will *not* remain so to the end: for the Lord and king of the earth is boundless love, justice, goodness itself, and He will thoroughly purge His floor, and cast out of His kingdom all things that offend, and make in His good time the kingdoms of this world, the kingdoms of God and of His Christ.'

'Ah but,' some one may say, 'that, if it ever happens at all, will not happen till we are dead, and what part or lot shall *we* have in it? we who die in the midst of all this sin, and injustice, and distress?' There again the Bible gives us hope: 'I believe,' says the Creed, 'in the resurrection of the flesh. The Bible teaches us to believe, that we, each of us, as human beings, men and women, shall have a share in that glorious day; not merely as ghosts, and disembodied spirits—of which the Bible, thanks be to God, says little or nothing, but as real live human beings, with new bodies of our own, on a new earth, under a new heaven. 'Therefore,' says David, 'my flesh shall rest in hope;' not merely my soul, my ghost, but my flesh. For the Lord, who not only died, but rose again with His body, shall raise our bodies, according to the mighty working by which He subdues all things to Himself; and then the whole manhood of each of us, body, soul, and spirit, shall have one perfect consummation and bliss, in His eternal and everlasting glory.—That is our hope. If that is not a gospel, and good news from heaven to poor distressed creatures in hovels, and on sick beds, to people racked with life-long pain and disease, to people in crowded cities, who never from week's end to week's end look on the green fields and bright sky—if that is not good news, and a dayspring of boundless hope from on high for them, what news can be?

But how are we to get this hope? The text tells us; through comfort of the Scriptures; through the strengthening and comforting promises, and examples, and rules of God's gracious dealings which we find therein. Through comfort of the Scriptures, but also through patience. Ah, my friends, of that too we must think; we must, as St. James says, 'let patience have her perfect work,' or else we shall not be perfect ourselves. If we are hasty, self-conceited, covetous, ready to help ourselves by the first means that come to hand; if we are full of hard judgments about our neighbours, and doubts about God's good purpose toward the world; in short, if we are not *patient*, the Bible will teach us little or nothing. It may make us superstitious, bigoted, fanatical, conceited, pharisaical, but like Jesus Christ the Lord it will not make us, unless we have patience.

And where are we to get patience? God knows it is hard in such a world as this for poor creatures to be patient always. But faith can breed patience, though patience cannot breed itself;—and faith in whom? Faith in our Father in heaven, even in the Almighty God Himself. He calls Himself 'the God of Patience and Consolation.' Pray for His Holy Spirit, and He will make you patient; pray for His Holy Spirit, and He will console and comfort you. He has promised That Spirit of His,

The Spirit of love, trust, and patience—The Comforter—to as many as ask Him. Ask Him now, this day—come to His holy table this day, and ask Him to make you patient; ask Him to take all the hastiness, and pride, and ill-temper, and self-will, and greediness out of you, and to change your wills into the likeness of His will. Then your eyes will be opened to understand His law. Then you will see in the Scriptures a sure promise of hope and glory and redemption for yourself and all the world. Then you will see in the blessed sacrament of the Lord's body and blood, a sure sign and warrant, handed down from land to land, and age to age, from year to year, and from father to son, that these promises shall come true; that hope shall become fact; that not one of the Lord's words shall fail, or pass away, till all be fulfilled.

III.

THE KINGDOM OF GOD.

THIRD SUNDAY IN ADVENT.

ISAIAH lxi. 1.

The Spirit of the Lord is upon me : because the Lord has anointed me to preach good tidings to the meek ; he has sent me to bind up the broken-hearted, to proclaim liberty to the captives, and the opening of the prison to them that are bound.

MY friends, I do entreat those of you who wish to get any real good from this sermon, to listen to me carefully all through it. Not that I have to complain of you in general for not attending to me. I thank God, and thank you, that you do listen to what is said in this pulpit. But there are many people who have a bad trick of minding the preacher carefully enough for a minute or two, and then letting their wits wander, and think about something else ; and then if any word in the sermon strikes them, waking up suddenly, and thinking again for a little, and then letting their thoughts run wild again ; and so on. Whereby it happens that they only recollect a few scraps of the sermon, a word here, and a sentence there, and get into their heads all sorts of mistakes and false notions about the preacher's meaning.

That is not right; that is not worthy of reasonable grown men: that is only pardonable in little scatterbrained children. Men and women should listen steadily, reverently throughout; so, and so only, will they be able to judge of the message which the preacher brings them. Listen to me, therefore, all through this sermon, and may God give you grace to understand it and lay it to heart, for it is the good news of the kingdom of God.

You recollect, I hope, that I have often told you, that the Lord Jesus Christ's words would never pass away; that His prophecies are continually coming true, and being fulfilled over and over again. Now this text is not one of His prophecies, but it is a prophecy about Him; one which He fulfilled, and which He has been fulfilling again and again. He is fulfilling it, as I believe, more than ever, now in these very days.

If you will look at the sixty-first chapter of Isaiah, you will find this prophecy; and you will find, too, what will surprise you at first, that Isaiah was speaking of himself. He says, 'that the Spirit of the Lord was upon *him*'—Isaiah—' because the Lord had appointed *him* to preach good tidings to the meek, to bind up the broken-hearted, and deliverance to the captives, to preach the acceptable year of the Lord.' Isaiah must have spoken truly about himself. He could not have meant to tell a falsehood, to say a thing was true of himself which was only true of Jesus, who did not come till 800 years afterwards. And he did speak the truth; you cannot read his prophecies without seeing that the Spirit of the Lord was indeed upon him; that the words which he spoke must have comforted all those who were sorrowing for their sins and the sins of the nation in their time. We know, for a fact, that his prophecies came true; that the Jewish captives were delivered and brought back out of Judæa to Jerusalem again, and that Jerusalem was rebuilt as Isaiah prophesied, and the Jewish nation raised to far greater holiness, and prosperity, and happiness, than it had ever been in before. And yet 800 years afterwards the Lord took those very same words to Himself and said, that *He* fulfilled them. He read them aloud once in a Jewish synagogue, out of the book of the prophet Isaiah; and then told the congregation, 'This day is this Scripture fulfilled in your ears.' And again, as we read in the Gospel for this day, when John the Baptist sent to ask Him if He was really the Christ, He made use of another prophecy of Isaiah, and told John's disciples that He *was* the Christ, because

THE KINGDOM OF GOD.

He was fulfilling that prophecy; because He was making the deaf hear, and the blind see, and preaching the gospel to the poor. Now how is that? Could Isaiah be right in applying those words to himself, and yet Christ be right in applying them to Himself? Can a prophecy be fulfilled twice over?

No doubt it can, my friends, and two hundred times over. No prophecy of Scripture is of private interpretation, says St. Peter. That is, it does not apply to any one private, particular thing that is to happen. Every prophecy of Scripture goes on fulfilling itself more and more, as time rolls on and the world grows older. St. Peter tells us the reason why. No prophecy of Scripture is of private interpretation; because it does not come from the will of man, from any invention or discovery of poor short-sighted human beings, who can only judge by what they see around them in their own times: but holy men of old spoke as they were moved by the Holy Spirit. And who is the Holy Spirit? The Spirit of God; the everlasting Spirit; the Spirit who cannot change, for He *is* God. The Spirit who searcheth the deep things of God, and teaches them to men. And what are the deep things of God? They are eternal as God is. Eternal laws; everlasting rules which cannot alter. That is the meaning of it all.

The Spirit of God is the spirit which teaches men the laws of God; the unchangeable rules and ordinances by which He governs all heaven and earth, and men, and nations; the laws which come into force, not once only, but always; the laws of God which are working round us now, just as much as they were eighteen hundred years ago, just as much as they were in Isaiah's time. Therefore it is, that I said that these old Jewish prophecies, which were inspired by the Holy Spirit, are coming true now, and will keep on coming true, time after time, in their proper place and order, and whensoever the times are fit for them, even to the end of the world.

But again, we read that the Spirit of God takes of the things of Christ, and shows them unto us. And what are the things of Christ? They must be eternal things, unchangeable things, for Christ is unchangeable—Jesus Christ, the same yesterday, to-day, and for ever. He is over all, God blessed for ever. To Him all power is given in heaven and earth. He reigns, and He will reign. Do you think He is less a Saviour now, than He was when he spoke those things to John's disciples? Do you think He is less able to hear and to help than He was in John's time? Do you think He used to care about people's bodies then, but that He only cares about their souls now? Do you think that He is less compassionate, and less merciful, as well as less powerful, than He was when He made the blind see, and the lame walk, and the deaf hear, in Judæa of old?

Less powerful! less compassionate! One would have expected that Christ was *more* powerful, *more* compassionate, if that were possible. At least one would expect that His power and compassion would show itself more and more, and make itself felt more and more, year by year, and age by age; more and more healing disease; more and more comforting sorrow; more and still more casting out cunning and evil spirits, till He had put all under His feet. He Himself said it should be so. He always spoke of His own kingdom, as a thing which was to grow and increase by laws of its own, men knew not how, but He knew. Like seed cast into the ground, His kingdom was, He said, at first the smallest of all seeds; but it was to grow, and take root, and spread into a mighty tree, He said, till the very birds in the air lodged in the branches of it; and David's words should be fulfilled, 'Thou, Lord, shalt save both man and beast.' And does not St. Paul speak of His kingdom in the same way, as a kingdom which should grow? that He was to reign till He had put all enemies under His feet? that He would deliver at last the whole creation? the earth on which we stand, the dumb animals around us? For, as St. Paul says, the whole creation is groaning in labour-pangs, waiting to be raised into a higher state. And it shall be raised. The whole creation shall be set free into the glorious liberty of the children of God.

What does that mean? How can I tell you?

This I can tell you, that it cannot mean that Jesus Christ was merciful enough to heal people's bodies at first, but that He has given up doing it now, and will never do it again. 'Well, but,' some would say, 'what does all this come to? You are merely telling us what we knew before—that if any of us are cured from disease, or raised up from a sick bed, it is all the Lord's doing.' If you do believe that, really, my friends, happy are you! Many of you, I think, *do* believe it. The poor are more inclined to believe it, I think, than the rich. But even in the mouths of the poor one often hears words which make one suspect that they do *not* believe it. I am very much afraid that a great many have got into the trick of saying, that it was God's mercy that they were cured, and that it pleased the Lord to raise them up from a sick bed, very much as a piece of cant. They say the words by rote, because they have been accustomed to hear them said by others, without thinking of the meaning of them; just as, on the other hand, a great many people curse and swear.

without thinking of the awful oaths they use. Ay, and often enough the very same persons will say that it was the Lord's mercy they were cured of their sickness; and then, if they get into a passion, pray the very same Lord to do that to the bodies and souls of their neighbours which it is a shame to speak of here. Out of the same mouth proceed blessings and cursings: showing that whether or not they are in earnest in cursing, they are not earnest in blessing.

Again:—If people really believed that it was the Lord Jesus Christ who cured their sicknesses for them, they would behave, when they got well, more as the Lord Jesus Christ would wish them to behave. They would show forth their thankfulness not only with their lips, but in their lives. You who believe—you who *say*—that Christ has cured your sicknesses, show your faith by your works. Live like those who are alive again from the dead; who are not your own, but bought with a price, and bound to work for God with your bodies and your spirits, which are His—*then*, and then only, can either God or man believe you.

Again:—There is a third reason which makes one suspect that people do not mean what they say about this matter. I think too many say, 'It has pleased God,' merely as an empty form of words, when all they mean is, 'What must be, must, and it cannot be helped.' Else, why do they say, 'It has pleased the Lord to send me sickness?' What is the use of saying, 'It has pleased the Lord to cure me,' when you say in the same breath, 'It has pleased the Lord to make me ill?' I know you will say that, 'Of course, whatever happens must be The Lord's will; if it did not please Him, it would not happen.' I do not care for such words; I will have nothing to do with them. I will neither entangle you nor myself in those endless disputings and questions about freewill and necessity, which never yet have come to any conclusion, and never will, because they are too deep for poor short-sighted human beings like us. 'To the law and to the testimony,' say I. I will hold to the words of the Bible; what it says, I will say; what it does not say I will *not* say, to please any man's system of doctrines. And I say from the Bible that we have no more right to say, 'It has pleased the Lord to make me sick,' than, 'It has pleased the Lord to make me a sinner.' Scripture everywhere speaks of sickness as a real evil and a curse—a breaking of the health, and order, and strength, and harmony of God's creation. It speaks of madmen as possessed with evil spirits; did *that* please God? The woman who was bowed with a spirit of infirmity, and could not lift herself up—did our Lord say that it had pleased God to make her a wretched cripple? No; he spoke of her as this daughter of Israel, whom Satan had bound, and not God, this eighteen years; and that was His reason for healing her, even on the sabbath-day, because her disease was not the work of God, but of the cruel, disordering, destroying evil spirit which is at enmity with God. That was why Christ cured her. And *that*—for this is the point I have been coming to, step by step—that was the reason why, when John the Baptist sent to ask if Jesus was the Christ, our Lord answered, 'Go and show John again those things which ye do see and hear: the blind receive their sight, and the lame walk, the lepers are cleansed, and the deaf hear, the dead are raised up, and the poor have the Gospel preached to them.'

Do not be in a hurry, my friends, and suppose that our Lord meant merely, 'Tell John what wonderful miracles I am working.' If He had meant that, why would He have put in as the last proof that He was the Christ, that He was preaching the Gospel to the poor? What wonderful miracle was there in *that?* No: it was as if He had said, 'Go and tell John that I am the Christ, because I am the great physician, the healer and deliverer of body and soul; one who will and can cure the loathsome diseases, the uselessness, the misery, the ignorance of the poorest and meanest.' He has proved Himself the Christ by showing not only His boundless power, but His boundless love and mercy; and *that*, not only to men's souls, but to their bodies also. To prove Himself the Christ by wonderful and astonishing miracles was exactly what He would *not* do. He refused, when the Scribes and Pharisees came and asked of Him a sign from heaven to prove that He was Christ— wanting Him, I suppose, to bring some apparition, or fiery comet, or great voice out of the sky, to astonish them with His power; He told them peremptorily that He would give them no such thing: and yet He said that His mighty works did prove Him to be Christ; He pronounced woe against Chorazin and Bethsaida for not believing Him on account of His mighty works: He told the Scribes and Pharisees that they ought to believe on Him merely for His works' sake. And why would they not believe on Him? Just because they could not see that God's power was shown more in healing and delivering sufferers, than in astonishing and destroying. They could not see that God's perfect likeness shone out in Christ—that He was the express image of the Father, just because He went about doing *good*, and healing all manner of sicknesses and all manner of infirmities among the people. But so it is, my friends! Jesus is the

Saviour, the deliverer, the great physician, the healer of soul and body. Not a pang is felt or a tear shed on earth, but He sorrows over it. Not a human being on earth dies young, but He, as I believe, sorrows over it. What it is which prevents Him healing every sickness, soothing every sorrow, wiping away every tear *now*, we cannot tell. But this we *can* tell, that it is His will that none should perish. This we *can* tell; that He is willing as ever to heal the sick, to cleanse the leper, to cast out devils, to teach the ignorant, to bind up the broken-hearted. This we *can* tell; that He will go on doing so more and more, year by year, and age by age. This we *can* tell; from Scripture, that Christ is stronger than the devil. This we *can* tell; that Christ, and all good men, the spirits of just men made perfect, the wise and the great in God's sight, who have left us their books, their sayings, their writings, as precious health-giving heirlooms —have been fighting, and are fighting, and will fight to the end against the devil, and sin, and oppression, and misery, and disease, and everything which spoils and darkens the face of God's good earth. And this we *can* tell; that they will conquer at the last, because Christ is stronger than the devil; good is stronger than evil; light is stronger than darkness: God's Spirit, the giver of life, and health, and order, is stronger than all the evil customs, and ignorance, and carelessness, and cruelty, and superstition, which makes miserable the lives, and, as far as we can see, destroys the souls, of thousands. Yes, I say, Christ's kingdom is a kingdom of health and deliverance for body and soul; and it will conquer; and it will spread; and it will grow, till the nations of the world have become the kingdoms of God and of His Christ. Christ reigns, and Christ will reign till He has put all His enemies under His feet; and the last of His enemies which shall be destroyed is *Death*. Death is His enemy. He has conquered death by rising from the dead. And the day will come when death will be no more—when sickness and sorrow shall be unknown, and God shall wipe away tears from all eyes. I say it again—never forget it— Christ is King, and His kingdom is a kingdom of health, and life, and deliverance from all evil. It always has been so, from the first time our Lord cured the leper in Galilee: it will be so to the end of the world. And, therefore—to come back to the very place from which I started at the beginning of my sermon—therefore, whenever one of the days of the Lord is at hand, whenever God's kingdom makes a great step forward, this same prophecy in our text is fulfilled in some striking and wonderful way. And I say it is fulfilled now in these days more than it ever has been. Christ is healing the sick, cleansing the leper, giving sight to the blind, raising the dead, and preaching the gospel to the poor, seven times more in these days in which we live than He did when He walked upon earth in Judæa.

Do you doubt my words? At all events you confess that the cure of all diseases comes from Christ. Then consider, I beseech you, how many more diseases are cured now than were formerly. One may say that the knowledge of medicine is not one hundred years old. Nothing, my friends, makes me feel more strongly what a wonderful and blessed time we live in, and how Christ is showing forth mighty works among us, than this same sudden miraculous improvement in the art of healing, which has taken place within the memory of man. Any country doctor now knows more, thank God, or ought to know, than the greatest London physicians did two generations ago. New cures for deafness, blindness, lameness, every disease that flesh is heir to, are being discovered year by year. Oh, my friends! you little know what Christ is doing among you, for your bodies as well as for your souls. There is not a parish in England now in which the poorest as well as the richest are not cured yearly of diseases, which, if they had lived a hundred years ago, would have killed them without hope or help. And then, when one looks at these great and blessed plans for what is called sanitary reform, at the sickness and the misery which has been done away with already by attending to them, even though they have only just begun to be put in practice,—our hearts must be hard indeed if we do not feel that Christ is revealing to us the gifts of healing far more bountifully and mercifully than even He did to the first apostles.

But you will say, perhaps, the dead are not raised in these days. Oh, my friends! which shows Christ's mercy most, to raise those who are already dead, or to save those alive who are about to die? Those in this church who have read history know as well as I, how in our forefathers' time people died in England by thousands of diseases which are scarcely ever deadly now; ay, of diseases which have now actually vanished out of the land, before the new light of medicine and of civilization which Christ has revealed to us in these days. For one child who lived and grew up in old times, two live and grow up now. In London alone there are not half as many deaths in proportion to the number of people as there were a hundred years ago. And is not that a mightier work of Christ's power and love than if He had raised a few dead persons to life?

And now for the last part of our Lord's witness

about Himself. To the poor the gospel is preached. Oh! my friends, is not *that* coming true in our days as it never came true before? Look back only fifty years, and consider the difference between the doctrines which were preached to the poor and the doctrines which are preached to them now. Look round you and see how everywhere earnest and godly ministers have sprung up, of all sects and opinions, as well as of the Church of England, not only to preach the gospel in the pulpit, but to carry it to the sick bedside of the lonely cottage, to the prison, and to those fearful sties, worse than prisons, where in our great cities the heathen poor live crowded together. Look at the teaching which the poor man can get now, compared to what he used to—the sermons, the Bibles, the tracts, the lending libraries, the schools,—just consider the hundreds of thousands of pounds which are subscribed every year to educate the children of the poor, and then say whether Christ is not working a mighty work among us in these days. I know that not half as much is done as ought to be done in that way; not half as much as will be done; and what is done will have to be done better than it has been done yet; but still can any one in this church who is fifty years old deny that there is a most enormous and blessed improvement which is growing and spreading every year? Can any one deny that the gospel is preached to the poor now in a way that it never was before within the memory of man?

Now, recollect that this is an Advent sermon—a sermon which proclaims to you that Christ is *come;* yes, He is come—come never to leave mankind again! Christ reigns over the earth, and will reign for ever. At certain great and important times in the world's history, like this present time, times which He himself calls 'days of the Lord,' He shows forth His power, and the mightiness and mercy of His kingdom, more than at others. But still He is always with us; we have no need to run up and down to look for Christ: to say, Who shall ascend into heaven to bring Him down? Who shall descend into the deep to bring Him up? For the kingdom of God, as He told us Himself, is among us, and within us. Yes, within us. All these wonderful improvements and discoveries, all things beneficial to men which are found out year by year, though they seem to be of men's invention, are really of Christ's revealing, the fruits of the kingdom of God within us, of the Spirit of God, who is teaching men, though they too often will not believe it; though they disclaim God's Spirit and take all the glory to themselves. Truly Christ is among us; and our eyes are held, and we see Him not. That is our English sin—the sin of unbelief, the root of every other sin. Christ works among us, and we will not own Him. Truly, Jesus Christ may well say of us English at this day, There were ten cleansed, but where are the nine? How few are there, who return to give glory to God! Oh, consider what I say; the kingdom of God is among us now; its blessings are growing richer, fuller among us every day. Beware, lest if we refuse to acknowledge that kingdom and Christ the King of it, it be taken away from us, and given to some other nation, who will bring forth the fruits of it, fellow-help and brotherly kindness, purity and sobriety, and all the fruits of the Spirit of God.

IV.

A PREPARATION FOR CHRISTMAS.

FOURTH SUNDAY IN ADVENT.

PHILIPPIANS iv. 4.

Rejoice in the Lord always.

THIS is the beginning of the Epistle for to-day, the Sunday before Christmas. We will try to find out why it was chosen for to-day, and what lesson we may learn from it.

Now Christmas-time was always a time of rejoicing among many heathen nations, and long before the Lord Jesus Christ came. That was natural and reasonable enough, if you will consider it. For now the shortest day is past. The sun is just beginning to climb higher and higher in the sky each day, and bring back with him longer sunshine, and shorter darkness, and spring flowers, and summer crops, and a whole new year, with new hopes, new work, new lessons, new blessings. The old year, with all its labours and all its pleasures, and all its sorrows and all its sins,

A PREPARATION FOR CHRISTMAS. 41

is dying, all but gone. It lies behind us, never to return. The tears which we shed, we never can shed again. The mistakes we made, we have a chance of mending in the year to come. And so the heathens felt, and rejoiced that another year was dying, another year going to be born.

And Christmas was a time of rejoicing too, because the farming work was done. The last year's crop was housed; the next year's wheat was sown; the cattle were safe in yard and stall; and men had time to rest, and draw round the fire in the long winter nights, and make merry over the earnings of the past year, and the hopes and plans of the year to come. And so over all this northern half of the world Christmas was a merry time.

But the poor heathens did not know the Lord. They did not know whom to thank for all their Christmas blessings. And so some used to thank the earth for the crops, and the sun for coming back again to lengthen the days, as if the earth and sun moved of themselves. And some used to thank false gods and ancient heroes, who, perhaps, never really lived at all. And some, perhaps the greater number, thanked nothing and no one, but just enjoyed themselves, and took no thought, as too many do now at Christmas-time. So the world went on, Christmas after Christmas; and the times of that ignorance, as St. Paul says, God winked at.

But when the fulness of time was come, He sent forth His Son, made of a woman, to be the judge and ruler of the world; and commanded all men everywhere to repent, and turn from all their vanities to serve the living God, who had made heaven and earth, and all things in them.

He did not wish them to give up their Christmas mirth. No: all along He had been trying to teach them by it about His love to them. As St. Paul told them once, God had not left Himself without witness, in that He gave them rain and fruitful seasons, filling their hearts with joy and gladness.

God did not wish them, or us, to give up Christmas mirth. The apostles did not wish it. The great men, true followers of the apostles, who shaped our Prayer-book for us, and sealed it with their life-blood, did not wish it. They did not wish farmers, labourers, servants, masters, to give up one of the old Christmas customs; but to remember who made Christmas, and its blessings; in short, to rejoice in The Lord. Our forefathers had been thanking the wrong persons for Christmas. Henceforward we were to thank the right person, The Lord, and rejoice in Him. Our forefathers had been rejoicing in the sun, and moon, and earth; in wise and valiant kings who had lived ages before; in their own strength and industry, and cunning. Now they were to rejoice in Him who made sun, and moon, and earth; in Him who sent wise and valiant kings and leaders; in Him who gives all strength, and industry, and cunning; by whose inspiration comes all knowledge of agriculture, and manufacture, and all the arts which raise men above the beasts that perish. So their Christmas joys were to go on, year by year, while the world lasted: but they were to go on rightly, and not wrongly. Men were to rejoice in The Lord, and then His blessing would be on them, and the thanks and praise which they offered Him, He would return with interest, in fresh blessings for the coming year.

Therefore, I think, this Epistle was chosen for to-day, the Sunday before Christmas, to show us in whom we are to rejoice; and, therefore, to show us how we are to rejoice. For we must not take the first verse of the Epistle and forget the rest. That would neither be wise nor reverent toward St. Paul, who wrote the whole, and meant the whole to stand together as one discourse; or to the blessed and holy men who chose it for our lesson on this day. Let us go on, then, with the Epistle, line by line, throughout.

'Rejoice in the Lord always, and again I say, rejoice.' As much as to say, you cannot rejoice too much, you cannot overdo your happiness, thankfulness, merriment. You do not know half—no, not the thousandth part of God's love and mercy to you, and you never will know. So do not be afraid of being too happy, or think that you honour God by wearing a sour face, when He is heaping blessings on you, and calling on you to smile and sing. But 'let your moderation be known unto all men.' There is a right and wrong way of being merry. There is a mirth, which is no mirth; whereof it is written, in the midst of that laughter there is a heaviness, and the end thereof is death. Drunkenness, gluttony, indecent words and jests and actions, these are out of place on Christmas-day, and in the merriment to which the pure and holy Lord Jesus calls you all. They are rejoicing in the flesh and the devil, and not in the Lord at all; and whosoever indulges in them, and fancies them merriment, is keeping the devil's Christmas, and not Jesus Christ's. So let your moderation be known to all men. Be *merry and wise.* The fool lets his mirth master him, and carry him away, till he forgets himself, and says and does things of which he is ashamed when he gets up next morning, sick and sad at heart. The wise man remembers that, let the occasion be as joyful a one as it may, 'the Lord is at hand.' Christ's eye is on him, while he is eating, and drinking, and laughing. He is not afraid of Christ's eye,

A PREPARATION FOR CHRISTMAS. 45

because, though it is Divine, it is a human, loving, smiling eye; rejoicing in the happiness of His poor, hard-worked brothers here below. But he remembers that it is a holy eye, too; an eye which looks with sadness and horror on anything which is wrong; on all drunkenness, quarrelling, indecency; and so in all his merriment, he is still master of himself. He remembers that his soul is nobler than his body; that his will must be stronger than his appetite; and so he keeps himself in check; he keeps his tongue from evil, and his stomach from sottishness, and though he may be, and ought to be, the merriest of the whole party, yet he takes care to let his moderation, his sobriety, be known and plain to every one, remembering that the Lord is at hand.

And that man—I will stand surety for him—will be the one who will rise from his bed next morning, best able to carry out the next verse of the Epistle, and 'be careful for nothing.'

Now that is no easy matter here in England; to rich and poor, Christmas is the time for settling accounts and paying debts. And therefore, in England, where living is dear, and every one, more or less, struggling to pay his way, Christmas is often a very anxious, disturbing time of year. Many a family, for all their economy, cannot clear themselves at the year's end; and though they are able to forget that now and then, thank God, through great part of the year, yet they cannot forget it at Christmas. But, as I said, the man who at Christmas-time will be most able to be careful for nothing, will be the man whose moderation has been known to every one; for he will, if he has lived the year through, in the same temper in which he has spent Christmas, have been moderate in his expenses; he will have kept himself from empty show, and pretending to be richer than he is. He will have kept himself from throwing away his money in drink, and kept his daughters from throwing away money in dress, which is just what too many, in their foolish, godless, indecent hurry to get rid of their own children off their hands, do not do.

And he will be the man who will be in the best humour, and have the clearest brain, to kneel down when he gets up to his daily work, and 'in everything, by prayer and supplication, make his requests known to God.' And then, whether he can make both ends meet or not, whether he can begin next year free from debt or not, still 'the peace of God will keep his heart.' He may be unable to clear himself, but still he will know, that he has a loving and merciful Father in heaven, who has allowed distress and difficulty to come on him, only as a lesson and an education. That this distress came because God chose, and that when God chooses, it will go away—and that till then—considering that the Lord God sent it—it had better *not* go away. He will believe that God's gracious promises stand true—that the Lord will never let those who trust in him be confounded and brought to shame—that he will let none of us be tempted beyond what we are able, but will always with the temptation make a way for us to escape, that we may be able to bear it. And so the peace of God which passes understanding, will keep that man's mind. And in whom? 'In Jesus Christ.' Now what did St. Paul mean by putting in the Lord Jesus Christ's name there? what is the meaning of 'in Jesus Christ?' This is what it means; it means what Christmas-day means. A man may say, 'Your sermon promises fine things, but I am miserable and poor; it promises a holy and noble rejoicing to every one, but I am unholy and mean. It promises peace from God, and I am sure I am not at peace: I am always fretting and quarrelling; I quarrel with my wife, my children, and my neighbours, and they quarrel with me; and worst of all,' says the poor man, 'I quarrel with myself. I am full of discontented, angry, sulky, anxious, unhappy thoughts; my heart is dark and sad and restless within me—would God I were peaceful, but I am not: look in my face and see!'

True, my friend, but on Christmas-day the Son of God was born into the world, a man like you.

'Well,' says the poor man, 'but what has that to do with my anxiety and my ill temper?'

It would take the whole year through, my friend, to show you all that it has to do with you and your unhappiness. All the Lessons, Epistles, and Gospels of the year, are set out to show you what it has to do with you. But in the meanwhile, before Christmas-day comes, consider this one thing—Why are you anxious? Because you do not know what is to happen to you? Then Christmas-day is a witness to you, that whatsoever happens to you, happens to you by the will and rule of Jesus Christ, The perfect man; think of that. *The perfect man*—who understands men's hearts, and wants, and all that is good for them, and has all the wisdom and power to give us what is good, which we want ourselves. And what makes you unhappy, my friends? Is it not at heart just this one thing—you are unhappy because you are not pleased with yourselves? And you are not pleased with yourselves, because you know you ought not to be pleased with yourselves; and you know you ought not to be pleased with yourselves, because you know, in the bottom of your hearts, that God is not pleased with you? What cure, what comfort for such thoughts can we find?—This.

The child who was born in a manger on Christmas-day, and grew up in poverty, and had not where to lay His head, went through all shame and sorrow to which man is heir. He, Jesus, the poor child of Bethlehem, is Lord and King of heaven and earth. He will feel for us; He will understand our temptations; He has been poor himself, that He might feel for the poor; He has been evil spoken of, that He might feel for those whose tempers are sorely tried. He bore the sins, and felt the miseries of the whole world, that He might feel for us, when we are wearied with the burden of life, and confounded by the remembrance of our own sins.

Oh, my friends, consider only Who was born into the world on Christmas-day; and that thought alone will be enough to fill you with rejoicing and hope for yourselves and all the world, and with the peace of God which passes understanding, the peace which the angels proclaimed to the shepherds on the first Christmas night—'On earth peace, and good will toward men'—and if God wills us good, my friends, what matter who wishes us evil?

V.

CHRISTMAS-DAY.

PHILIPPIANS ii. 7.

He made himself of no reputation, and took upon him the form of a slave.

ON Christmas-day, 1851 years ago, if we had been at Rome, the great capital city, and mistress of the whole world, we should have seen a strange sight—strange, and yet pleasant. All the courts of law were shut; no war was allowed to be proclaimed, and no criminals punished. The sorrow and the strife of that great city had stopped, in great part, for three days, and all people were giving themselves up to merriment and good cheer—making up quarrels, and giving and receiving presents from house to house. And we should have seen, too, a pleasanter sight even than that. For those three days of Christmas-time were days of safety and merriment for the poor slaves—tens of thousands of whom, men, women, and children, the Romans had brought out of all the countries in the world—many of our forefathers and mothers among them—and kept them there in cruel bondage and shame, worked and fed, bought and sold, like beasts, and not like human beings, not able to call their lives or their bodies their own, forced to endure any shame or sin which their tyrants required of them, and liable any moment to be beaten, tortured, or crucified at the mercy of cruel and foul masters and mistresses. But on that Christmas-day, according to an old custom, they were allowed for once in the whole year to play at being free, to dress in their masters' and mistresses' clothes, to say what they thought of them boldly, without fear of punishment, and to eat and drink at their masters' tables, while their masters and mistresses waited on them. It was an old custom, that, among the heathen Romans, which their forefathers, who were wiser and better than they, had handed down to them. They had forgotten, perhaps, what it meant: but still we may see what it must have meant—That the old forefathers of the Romans had intended to remind their children every year by that custom, that their poor hard-worked slaves were, after all, men and women as much as their masters; that they had hearts and consciences, and sense in them, and a right to speak what they thought, as much as their masters; that they, as much as their masters, could enjoy the good things of God's earth, from which man's tyranny had shut them out; and to remind those cruel masters, by making them once every year wait on their own slaves at table, that they were, after all, equal in the sight of God, and that it was more noble for those who were rich, and called themselves gentlemen, to help others, than to make others slave for them.

I do not mean, of course, that those old heathens understood all this clearly. You will see, by the latter part of my sermon, why they could not understand it clearly. But there must have been some sort of dim, confused suspicion in their minds that it was wrong and cruel to treat human beings like brute beasts, which made them set up that strange old custom of letting their slaves play at being free, once every Christmas-tide.

But if on this same day, 1851 years ago, instead of being in the great city of Rome, we had been in the little village of Bethlehem in Judæa, we might have seen a sight stranger still; a sight which we could not have fancied had anything to do with that merry-making of the slaves at Rome, and yet which had everything to do with it.

We should have seen, in a mean stable, among the oxen and the asses, a poor maiden, with her new-born baby laid in the manger, for want of any better cradle, and by her her husband, a poor carpenter, whom all men thought to be the father of her child. . . There, in the stable, amid the straw, through the cold winter days and nights, in want of many a comfort which the poorest woman, and the poorest woman's child would need, they stayed there, that young maiden and her new-born babe. . . . That young maiden was the Blessed Virgin Mary, and that poor baby was the Son of God. The Son of God, in whose likeness all men were made at the beginning; the Son of God, who had been ruling the whole world all along; who brought the Jews out of slavery, a thousand years before, and destroyed their cruel tyrants in the Red Sea; the Son of God, who had been all along punishing cruel tyrants and oppressors, and helping the poor out of misery, whenever they called on him. The Light which lightens every man who comes into the world, was that poor babe. It was He who gives men reason, and conscience, and a tender heart, and delight in what is good, and shame and uneasiness of mind when they do wrong. It was He who had been stirring up, year by year, in those cruel Romans' hearts, the feeling that there was something wrong in grinding down their slaves, and put into their minds the notion of giving them their Christmas rest and freedom. He had been keeping up that good old custom for a witness and a warning that all men were equal in His sight; that all men had a right to liberty of speech and conscience; a right to some fair share in the good things of the earth, which God had given to all men freely to enjoy. But those old Romans would not take the warning. They kept up the custom, but they shut their eyes to the lesson of it. They went on conquering and oppressing all the nations of the earth, and making them their slaves. And now He was come—He Himself, the true Lord of the earth, the true pattern of men. He was come to show men to whom this world belonged : He was come to show men in what true power, true nobleness consisted—not in making others minister to us, but in ministering to them : He was come to set a pattern of what a man should be; He was the Son of Man—THE MAN of all men—and therefore He had come with good news to all poor slaves, and neglected, hardworked creatures : He had come to tell them that He cared for them ; that He could and would deliver them; that they were God's children, and His brothers, just as much as their Roman masters; and that He was going to bring a terrible time upon the earth—" days of the Son of Man," when He would judge all men, and show who were true men and who were not—such a time as had never been before, or would be again; when that great Roman empire, in spite of all its armies, and its cunning, and its riches, plundered from every nation under heaven, would crumble away and

CHRISTMAS-DAY. 55

perish shamefully and miserably off the face of the earth, before tribes of poor, untaught, savage men, the brothers and countrymen of those very slaves whom the Romans fancied were so much below them, that they had a right to treat them like the beasts which perish.

That was the message which that little child lying in the manger there at Bethlehem, had been sent out from God to preach. Do you not see now what it had to do with that strange merrymaking of the poor slaves in Rome, which I showed you at the beginning of my sermon?

If you do not, I must remind you of the song, which, St. Luke says, the shepherds in Judæa heard the angels sing, on this night 1851 years ago. That song tells us the meaning of that babe's coming. That song tells us what that babe's coming had to do with the poor slaves of Rome, and with all poor creatures who have suffered and sorrowed on this earth, before or since.

'Glory to God in the highest,' they sang, 'and on earth peace, good will to men.'

Glory to God in the highest. That little babe, lying in the manger among the cattle, was showing what was the very highest glory of the great God who had made heaven and earth. Not to show His power and His majesty, but to show His condescension and His love. To stoop, to condescend, to have mercy, to forgive, that is the highest glory of God. That is the noblest, the most Godlike thing for God or man. And God showed that when he sent down his only-begotten Son—not to strike the world to atoms with a touch, not to hurl sinners into everlasting flame, but to be born of a village maiden, to take on Himself all the shame and weakness and sorrow, to which man is heir, even to death itself; to make Himself of no reputation, and take on Himself the form of a slave, and forgive sinners, and heal the sick, and comfort the outcast and despised, that He might show what God was like—show forth to men, as a poor maiden's son, the brightness of God's glory, and the express likeness of His person.

'And on earth peace' they sang. Men had been quarrelling and fighting then, and men are quarrelling and fighting now. That little babe in the manger was come to show them how and why they were all to be at peace with each other. For what causes all the war and quarrelling in the world, but selfishness? Selfishness breeds pride, passion, spite, revenge, covetousness, oppression. The strong care for themselves, and try to help themselves at the expense of the weak, by force and tyranny; the weak care for themselves in their turn, and try to help themselves at the expense of the strong, by cunning and cheating. No one will condescend, give way, sacrifice his own interest for his neighbour's, and hence come wars between nations, quarrels in families, spite and grudges between neighbours. But in the example of that little child of Bethlehem, Jesus Christ the Lord, God was saying to men, 'Acquaint yourselves with Me, and be at peace.' God is not selfish; it is our selfishness which has made us unlike God. God so loved the sinful world, that He gave His only-begotten Son for it. Is that an action like ours? The Son of God so obeyed His Father, and so loved this world, that He made Himself of no reputation, and took on Him the likeness of a slave, and became obedient to death, even to the most fearful and shameful of all deaths, the death of the cross; not for Himself, but for those who did not know Him, hated Him, killed Him. In short, He sacrificed Himself for us. That is God's likeness. Self-sacrifice. Jesus Christ, the babe of Bethlehem, proved Himself the Son of God, and the express likeness of the Father, by sacrificing Himself for us. Sacrifice yourselves then for each other! Give up your own pride, your own selfishness, your own interest for each other, and you will be all at peace at once.

But the angels sang, 'Good will toward men.' Without that their song would not have been complete. For we are all ready to say, at such words as I have been speaking, 'Ah! pleasant enough, and pretty enough, if they were but possible; but they are not possible. It is in the nature of man to be selfish. Men have gone on warring, grudging, struggling, competing, oppressing, cheating from the beginning, and they will do so to the end.'

Yes, it is not in the *nature* of man to do otherwise. In as far as man yields to his nature, and is like the selfish brute beasts, it is not possible for him to do anything but go on quarrelling, and competing, and cheating to the last. But what man's nature cannot do, God's grace can. God's good will is toward you. He loves you, He wills —and if He wills, what is too hard for him?—He wills to raise you out of this selfish, quarrelsome life of sin, into a loving, brotherly, peaceful life of righteousness. His spirit, the spirit of love by which He made and guides all heaven and earth, the spirit of love in which He gave His only Son for you, the spirit of love in which His Son Jesus Christ sacrificed Himself for you, and took on Himself a meaner state than any of you can ever have—the likeness of a slave—that spirit is promised to you, and ready for you. That little baby in the manger at Bethlehem—God sacrificing Himself for you in the spirit of love—is a sign that that spirit of love is the spirit of God, and therefore the only right spirit for you and me, who are men and women made in the image of God. That babe in the manger at Bethlehem is a sign to you and me, that God will freely give us that spirit of love if we ask for it. For He would not have set us that example, if He had not meant us to follow it, and He would not ask us to follow it, if He did not intend to give us the means of following it. Therefore, my friends, it is written, Ask and ye shall receive. If your heavenly Father spared not His own Son, but freely gave Him for you, will He not with Him likewise freely give you all things? Oh! ask, and you shall receive. However poor, ignorant, sinful you may be, God's promises are ready for you, signed and sealed by the bread and wine on that table, the memorial of Jesus, the babe of Bethlehem. Ask, and you shall receive! Comfort from sorrow, peaceful assurance of God's good will toward you, deliverance from your sins, and a share in the likeness of Him who on this day made himself of no reputation, and took on him the form of a slave.

VI.

TRUE ABSTINENCE.

FIRST SUNDAY IN LENT.

1 CORINTHIANS ix. 27.

I keep under my body, and bring it into subjection.

IN the Collect for this day we have just been praying to God, to give us grace to use such abstinence, that our flesh being subdued to our spirit, we may follow his godly motions.

Now we ought to have meant something when we said these words. What did we mean by them? Perhaps some of us did not understand them They could not be expected to mean anything by them. But it is a sad thing, a very sad thing, that people will come to church Sunday after Sunday, and repeat by rote words which they do not understand, words by which they therefore mean nothing, and yet never care or try to understand them.

What are the words there for, except to be understood? All of you call people foolish, who submit to have prayers read in their churches in a foreign language, which none, at least of the poor, can understand. But what right have you to call them foolish, if you, whose Prayer-books are written in English, take no trouble to find out the meaning of them? Would to Heaven that you would try to find out the meaning of the Prayer-book! Would to Heaven that the day would come, when any one in this parish who was puzzled by any doctrine of religion, or by any text in the Bible, or word in the Prayer-book, would come confidently to me, and ask me to explain it to him! God knows, I should think it an honour and a pleasure, as well as a duty. I should think no time better spent than in answering your questions. I do beseech you to ask me, every one of you, when and where you like, any questions about religion which come into your minds. Why am I put in this parish, except to teach you? and how can I teach you better, than by answering your questions? As it is, I am disheartened, and all but hopeless, at times, about the state of this parish, and the work I am trying to do here; because, though you will come and hear me, thank God, willingly enough, you do not seem yet to have gained confidence enough in me, or to have learnt to care sufficiently about the best things, to ask questions of me about them. My dear friends, if you wanted to get information about anything you really cared for, you would ask questions enough. If you wanted to know some way to a place on earth you would ask it; why not ask your way to things better than this earth can give? But whether or not you will question me I must go on preaching to you, though whether or not you care to listen is more, alas! than I can tell.

But listen to me, now, I beseech you, while I try to explain to you the meaning of the words which you have been just using in this collect. You have asked God to give you grace to use abstinence. Now what is the meaning of abstinence? Abstinence means abstaining, refraining, keeping back of your own will from doing something which you might do. Take an example. When a man for his health's sake, or his purse's sake, or any other good reason, drinks less liquor than he might if he chose, he abstains from liquor. He uses abstinence about liquor. There are other things in which a man may abstain. Indeed, he may abstain from doing anything he likes. He may abstain from eating too much; from lying in bed too long; from reading too much; from taking too much pleasure; from making money; from spending money; from right things; from wrong things; from things which are neither right nor wrong; on all these he may use abstinence. He may abstain for many reasons; for good ones, or for bad ones. A miser will abstain from all sorts of comforts, to hoard up money. A superstitious man may abstain from comforts, because he thinks God grudges them to him, or because he thinks God is pleased by the unhappiness of his creatures, or because he has been taught, poor wretch, that if he makes himself uncomfortable in this life, he shall have more comfort, more honour, more reason for pride and self-glorification, in the life to come. Or a man may abstain from one pleasure, just to be able to enjoy another all the more ; as some great gamblers drink nothing but water, in order to keep their heads clear for cheating. All these are poor reasons ; some of them base, some of them wicked reasons for abstaining from anything. Therefore, abstinence is not a good thing in itself; for if a thing is good in itself, it can never be wrong. Love is good in itself, and, therefore, you cannot love any one for a bad reason. Justice is good in itself, pity is good in itself, and, therefore, you can never be wrong in being just or pitiful.

But abstinence is not a good thing in itself. If it were, we should all be bound to abstain always from everything pleasant, and make ourselves as miserable and uncomfortable as possible, as some superstitious persons used to do in old times. Abstinence is only good when it is used for a good reason. If a man abstains from pleasure himself, to save up for his children; if he abstains from over eating and over drinking, to keep his mind clear and quiet; if he abstains from sleep and ease, in order to have time to see his business properly done; if he abstains from spending money on himself, in order to spend it for others; if he abstains from any habit, however harmless or pleasant, because he finds it lead him towards what is wrong, and put him into temptation; then he does right; then he is doing God's work; then he may expect God's blessing; then he is trying to do what we all prayed God to help us to do, when we said, 'Give us grace to use such abstinence;' then he is doing, more or less, what St. Paul says he did, 'Keeping his body under, and bringing it into subjection.'

For, see, the Collect does not say, 'Give us grace to use abstinence,' as if abstinence were a good thing in itself, but 'to use such abstinence, that'— to use a certain kind of abstinence, and that for a certain purpose, and that purpose a good one; such abstinence that our flesh may be subdued to our spirit; that our flesh, the animal, bodily nature which is in us, loving ease and pleasure, may not be our master, but our servant; so that we may not follow blindly our own appetites, and do just what we like, as brute beasts which have no understanding. And our flesh is to be subdued to our spirit for a certain purpose; not because our flesh is bad, and our spirit good; not in order that we may puff ourselves up and admire ourselves, and say, as the philosophers among the heathen used, 'What a strong-minded, sober, self-restraining man I am! How fine it is to be able to look down on my neighbours, who cannot help being fond of enjoying themselves, and cannot help caring for this world's good things. I am above all that. I want nothing, and I feel nothing, and nothing can make me glad or sorry. I am master of my own mind, and own no law but my own will.' The Collect gives us the true and only reason, for which it is right to subdue our appetites; which is, that we may keep our minds clear and strong enough to listen to the voice of God within our hearts and reasons; to obey the motions of God's Spirit in us; not to make our bodies our masters, but to live as God's servants.

This is St. Paul's meaning, when he speaks of keeping under his body, and bringing it into subjection. The exact word which he uses, however, is a much stronger one than merely 'keeping under;' it means simply, to beat a man's face black and blue; and his reason for using such a strong word about the matter is, to show us that he thought no labour too hard, no training too sharp, which teaches us how to restrain ourselves, and keep our appetites and passions in manful and godly control.

Now, a few verses before my text, St. Paul takes an example from foot racers. 'These foot racers,' he says, 'heathens though they are, and only trying to win a worthless prize, the petty honour of a crown of leaves, see what trouble they take; how they exercise their limbs; how careful and temperate they are in eating and drinking, how much pain and fatigue they go through to get themselves into perfect training for a race. How much more trouble ought we take, to make ourselves fit to do God's work? For these foot racers do all this only to gain a garland, which will wither in a week; but we, to gain a garland which will never fade away; a garland of holiness, and righteousness, and purity, and the likeness of Jesus Christ.'

The next example of abstinence which St. Paul takes, is from the prize-fighters, who were very numerous and very famous, in the country in which the Corinthians lived. 'I fight,' he says, 'not like one who beats the air;' that is, not like a man who is only brandishing his hands, and sparring in jest, but like a man who knows that he has a fight to fight in hard earnest; a terrible life-long fight against sin, the world, and the devil; 'and, therefore,' he says, 'I do as these fighters do.' They, poor savage and brutal heathens as they are, go through a long and painful training. Their very practice is not play; it is grim earnest. They stand up to strike, and be struck, and are bruised and disfigured as a matter of course, in order that they may learn not to flinch from pain, or lose their tempers, or turn cowards, when they have to fight. 'And so do I,' says St. Paul; 'they, poor men, submit to painful and disagreeable things to make them brave in their paltry battles. I submit to painful and disagreeable things, to make me brave in the great battle which I have to fight against sin, and ignorance, and heathendom.' 'Therefore,' he says, in another place, 'I take pleasure in afflictions, in persecutions, in necessities, in distresses;' and that not because those things were pleasant, they were just as unpleasant to him as to any one else; but because they taught him to bear, taught him to be brave; taught him, in short, to become a perfect man of God.

This is St. Paul's account of his own training: in the Epistle for to-day, we have another account of it; a description of the life which he led, and which he was content to lead—'in much suffering, in stripes, in imprisonments, in tumults, in labours, in watchings, in fastings'—and an account, too, of the temper which he had learnt to show amid such a life of vexation, and suffering, and shame, and danger—'approving himself in all things the minister of God, by pureness, by wisdom, by long suffering, by kindness, by the spirit of holiness, by love unfeigned;' 'as dying, and behold we live; as chastened, and not killed; as sorrowful, yet always rejoicing; as poor, yet making many rich; as having nothing, yet possessing all things.'— In all things proving himself a true messenger from God, by being able to dare and to endure for God's sake, what no man ever would have dared and endured for his own sake.

'But'—some one may say,—'St. Paul was an apostle; he had a great work to do in the world; he had to turn the heathen to God; and it is likely enough that he required to train himself, and keep strict watch over all his habits, and ways of thinking and behaving, lest he should grow selfish, lazy, cowardly, covetous, fond of ease and amusement. He had, of course, to lead a life of strange suffering and danger; and he had therefore to train himself for it. But what need have we to do as St. Paul did?'

Just as much need, my good friends, if you could see it.

Which of us has not to lead a life of suffering? We shall each and all of us, have our full share of trouble before we die, doubt it not.

TRUE ABSTINENCE.   69

And which of us has not to lead a life of danger? I do not mean bodily danger; of that, there is little enough—perhaps too little—in England now; but of danger to our hearts, minds, characters? Oh, my friends, I pity those who do not think themselves in danger every day of their lives, for the less danger they see around them, the more danger there is. There is not only the common danger of temptation, but over and above it, the worse danger of not knowing temptation when it comes. Who will be most likely to walk into pits and mires upon the moor—the man who knows that they are there around him, or the man who goes on careless and light of heart, fancying that it is all smooth ground? Woe to you, young people, if you fancy that you are to have no woe! Danger to you, young people, if you fancy yourselves in no danger!

'This is sad and dreary news'—some of you may say. Ay, my friends, it would be sad and dreary news indeed; and this earth would be a very sad and dreary place; and life with all its troubles and temptations, would not be worth having, if it were not for the blessed news which the Gospel for this day brings us. That makes up for all the sadness of the Epistle; that gives us hope; that tells us of one who has been through life, and through death too, yet without sin. That tells us of one who has endured a thousand times more temptation than we ever shall, a thousand times more trouble than we ever shall, and yet has conquered it all; and that He who has thus been through all our temptations, borne all our weaknesses, is our King, our Saviour, who loves us, who teaches us, who has promised us His Holy Spirit, to make us like Himself, strong, brave, and patient, to endure all that man or devil, or our own low animal tempers and lusts, can do to hurt us. The Gospel for this day tells us how He went and was alone in the wilderness with the wild beasts, and yet trusted in God, His Father and ours, to keep Him safe. How He went without food forty days and nights, and yet in His extreme hunger, refused to do the least self-willed or selfish thing to get Himself food. Is that no lesson, no message of hope for the poor man who is tempted by hunger to steal, or tempted by need to do a mean and selfish thing, to hear that the Lord Jesus Christ, who bore need and hunger far worse than his, understands all his temptations, and feels for him, and pities him, and has promised him God's Spirit, to make him strong, as He himself was?

Is it no comfort to young people who are tempted to vanity, and display, and self-willed conceited longings, tempted to despise the advice of their parents and elders, and set up for themselves, and choose their own way—Is it no good news, I say, for them to hear that their Lord and Saviour was tempted to it also, and conquered it ?—That He will teach them to answer the temptation as He did, when he refused even to let angels hold Him over the temple, up between earth and heaven, for a sign and a wonder to all the Jews, because God His Father had not bidden Him to do it, and therefore He would not tempt the Lord His God.

Is it no good news, again, to those who are tempted to do perhaps one little outward wrong thing, to yield on some small point to the ways of the world, in order to help themselves on in life, to hear that their Lord and Saviour conquered that temptation too ?—That He refused all the kingdoms of the world, and the glory of them, when the devil offered them, because He knew that the devil could not give them to Him ; that all wealth, and power, and glory belonged to God, and was to be got only by serving Him.

Oh do you all, young people especially, think of this. As you grow up and go out into life, you will be tempted in a hundred different ways, by things which are pleasant—every one knows that they are pleasant enough—but wrong. One will be tempted to be vain of dress ; another to be self-conceited : another to be lazy and idle ; another to be extravagant and roving; another to be over fond of amusement; another to be over fond of money; another to be over fond of liquor; another to go wrong, as too many young men and young women do, and bring themselves, and those with whom they keep company, and whom they ought, if they really love them, to respect and honour, down into sin and shame. You will all be tempted, and you will all be troubled; one by poverty, one by sickness, one by the burden of a family, one by being laughed at for trying to do right.—But remember, oh, remember, whenever a temptation comes upon you, that The blessed Jesus has been through it all, and conquered all, and that His will is, that you shall be holy and pure like Him, and that, therefore, if you but ask Him, He will give you strength to keep pure. When you are tempted, pray to Him: the struggle in your own minds will, no doubt, be very great; it will be very hard work for you—sin looks so pleasant on the outside! Poor souls, it is a sad struggle for you! Many a poor young fellow, who goes wrong, deserves rather to be pitied than to be punished. Well then, if no man else will pity him, Jesus, the Man of all men, will. Pray to Him! Cry aloud to Him! Ask Him to make you stout-hearted, patient, really manful, to fight against temptation. Ask Him to give you strength of mind to fight against all bad habits. Ask Him to open your eyes to see when you are in danger. Ask Him to help you to keep out of the way of temptation. Ask Him, in short, to give you grace to use such abstinence that your flesh may be subdued to your spirit. And then you will not follow, as the beasts do, just what seems pleasant to your flesh; no, you will be able to obey Christ's godly motions, that is, to do, as well as to love, the good desires which He puts into your hearts. You will do not merely what is pleasant, but what is right; you will not be your own slaves, you will be your own masters, and God's loyal and obedient sons; you will not be, as too many are, mere animals going about in the shape of men, but truly men at heart, who are not afraid of pain, poverty, shame, trouble, or death itself, when they are in the right path, about the work to which God has called them.

But if you ask Christ to make true men and women of you, you must believe that He will give you what you ask; if you ask Him to help you, you must believe that He will and does help you— you must believe that it is He himself who has put into your hearts the very desire of being holy and strong at all; and therefore you must believe that you can help yourselves. Help yourselves, and He will help you. If you ask for His help, He will give it. But what is the use of His giving it, if you do not use it? To him who has shall be given, and he shall have more; but from him who has not shall be taken away even what he seems to have. Therefore do not merely pray, but struggle and try *yourselves*. Train yourselves as St. Paul did; train yourselves to keep your temper; train yourselves to bear unpleasant things for the sake of your duty; train yourselves to keep out of temptation; train yourselves to be forgiving, gentle, thrifty, industrious, sober, temperate, cleanly, as modest as little children in your words, and thoughts, and conduct. And God, when He sees you trying to be all this, will help you to be so. It may be hard to educate yourselves. Life is a hard business at best —you will find it a thousand times harder, though, if you are slaves to your own fleshly sins. But the more you struggle against sin, the less hard you will find it to fight; the more you resist the devil, the more he will flee from you; the more you try to conquer your own bad passions, the more God will help you to conquer them; it may be a hard battle, but it is a sure one. No fear but that every one can, if he will, work out his own salvation, for it is God Himself who works in us to will and to do of His good pleasure. All you have to do is to give yourselves up to Him, to study His laws, to labour as well as long to keep them, and He will enable you to keep them; He will teach you in a thousand unexpected ways; He will daily renew and strengthen your hearts by the working of His Spirit, that you may more and more know, and love, and do, what is right; and you will go on from strength to strength, to the height of perfect men, to the likeness of Jesus Christ the Lord, who conquered all human temptations for your sake, that He might be a high-priest who can be touched with the feeling of our infirmities, because He was tempted in all points like as we are, yet without sin.

VII.

GOOD FRIDAY.

ISAIAH lxiii. 9.

In all their affliction He was afflicted, and the angel of His presence saved them. In His love and in His pity He redeemed them; and He bare them and carried them all the days of old.

ON this very day, at this very hour, 1817 years ago, hung one nailed to a cross; bruised and bleeding, pierced and naked, dying a felon's death between two thieves; in perfect misery, in utter shame, mocked and insulted by all the great, the rich, the learned of his nation; one who had grown up as a man of low birth, believed by all to be a carpenter's son; without scholarship, money, respectability; even without a home wherein to lay His head—and here was the end of His life! True, He had preached noble words, He had done noble deeds: but what had they helped Him? They had not made the rich, the learned, the respectable, the religious believe on Him; they had not saved Him from persecution, and insult, and death. The only mourners who stood by to weep over His dying agonies were His mother, a poor countrywoman; a young fisherman; and one who had been a harlot and a sinner. There was an end!

Do you know who that Man was? He was your King; the King of rich and poor; and He was your King, not in spite of His suffering all that shame and misery, but just because He suffered it; because He chose to be poor, and miserable, and despised; because He endured the cross, despising the shame; because He took upon Himself, to fulfil His Father's will, all ills which flesh is heir to—therefore He is now your King, the Saviour of the world, the poor man's friend, the Lord of heaven and earth. Is He such a King as *you* wish for?

Is He the sort of King you want, my friends? Does He fulfil your notions of what the poor man's friend should be? Do you, in your hearts, wish He had been somewhat richer, more glorious, more successful in the world's eyes—a wealthy and prosperous man, like Solomon of old? Are any of you ready to say, as the money-blinded Jews said, when they demanded their true King to be crucified, 'We have no king but Cæsar?—Provided the law-makers and the authorities take care of our interests, and protect our property, and do not make us pay too many rates and taxes, that is enough for us.' Will you have no king but Cæsar?

Alas! those who say that, find that the law is but a weak deliverer, too weak to protect them from selfishness, and covetousness, and decent cruelty; and so Cæsar and the law have to give place to Mammon, the god of money. Do we not see it in these very days? And Mammon is weak, too. This world is not a shop, men are not merely money-makers and wages-earners. There are more things in heaven and earth than are dreamt of in that sort of philosophy. Self-interest and covetousness cannot keep society orderly and peaceful, let sham philosophers say what they will. And then comes tyranny, lawlessness, rich and poor staining their hands in each other's blood, as we saw happen in France two years ago; and so, after all, Mammon has to give place to Moloch, the fiend of murder and cruelty; and woe to rich and poor when he reigns over them! Ay, woe—woe to rich and poor when they choose any one for their king but their real and rightful Lord and Master, Jesus, the poor man, afflicted in all their afflictions, the Man of sorrows, crucified on this day.

Is He the kind of King you like? Make up your minds, my friends—make up your minds! For whether you like Him or not, your King He was, your King He is, your King He will be, blessed be God, for ever. Blessed be God, indeed! If He were not our King; if any one in heaven or earth was Lord of us, except the Man of sorrows, the Prince of sufferers, what hope, what comfort would there be? What a horrible, black, fathomless riddle this sad, diseased, moaning world would be! No king will suit us but the Prince of sufferers—Jesus, who has borne all this world's griefs, and carried all its sorrows—Jesus, who has Himself smarted under pain and hunger, oppression and insult, treachery and desertion, who knows them all, feels for them all, and will right them all, in His own good time.

Believing in Jesus, we can travel on, through one wild parish after another, upon English soil, and see, as I have done, the labourer who tills the land worse housed than the horse he drives, worse clothed than the sheep he shears, worse nourished than the hog he feeds—and yet not despair: for the Prince of Sufferers is the labourer's Saviour; He has tasted hunger, and thirst, and weariness, poverty, oppression, and neglect; the very tramp who wanders houseless on the moor-side is His brother; in his sufferings the Saviour of the world has shared, when the foxes had holes, and the birds of the air had nests, while the Son of God had not where to lay His head. He is the King of the poor, firstborn among many brethren; His tenderness is Almighty, and for the poor He has prepared deliverance, perhaps in this world, surely in the world to come—boundless deliverance, out of the treasures of His boundless love.

Believing in Jesus, we can pass by mines, and factories, and by dungeons darker and fouler still, in the lanes and alleys of our great towns and cities, where thousands and tens of thousands of starving men, and wan women, and children grown old before their youth, sit toiling and pining in Mammon's prison-house, in worse than Egyptian bondage, to earn such pay as just keeps the broken heart within the worn-out body;—ay, we can go through our great cities, even now, and see the women, whom God intended to be Christian wives and mothers, the slaves of the rich man's greed by day, the playthings of his lust by night—and yet not despair: for we can cry, No! thou proud Mammon, money-making fiend! These are not thine, but Christ's; they belong to Him who died on the cross; and though thou heedest not their sighs, He marks them all, for He has sighed like them; though there be no pity in thee, there is in Him the pity of a man, ay, and the indignation of a God! He treasures up their tears; He understands their sorrows; His judgment of their guilt is not like thine, thou Pharisee! He is their Lord, who said, that to those to whom little was given, of them shall little be required. Generation after generation, they are being made perfect by

GOOD FRIDAY. 81

sufferings, as their Saviour was before them; and then, woe to thee! For even as he led Israel out of Egypt with a mighty hand, and a stretched-out arm, and signs and wonders, great and terrible, so shall He lead the poor out of their misery, and make them households like a flock of sheep; even as He led Israel through the wilderness, tender, forbearing, knowing whereof they were made, having mercy on all their brutalities, and idolatries, murmurings, and backslidings, afflicted in all their afflictions—even while He was punishing them outwardly, as He is punishing the poor man now— even so shall He lead this people out in His good time, into a good land and large, a land of wheat and wine, of milk and honey; a rest which He has prepared for His poor, such as eye hath not seen, nor ear heard, nor hath it entered into the heart of man to conceive. He can do it; for the Almighty Deliverer is His name. He will do it; for His name is Love. He knows how to do it; for He has borne the griefs, and carried the sorrows of the poor.

Oh, sad hearts and suffering! Anxious and weary ones! Look to the cross this day! There hung your king! The King of sorrowing souls, and more, the King of sorrows. Ay, pain and grief, tyranny and desertion, death and hell, He has faced them one and all, and tried their strength, and taught them His, and conquered them right royally!

And, since He hung upon that torturing cross, sorrow is divine, godlike, as joy itself. All that man's fallen nature dreads and despises, God honoured on the cross, and took unto Himself, and blest, and consecrated for ever. And now, blessed are the poor, if they are poor in heart, as well as purse; for Jesus was poor, and theirs is the kingdom of heaven. Blessed are the hungry, if they hunger for righteousness as well as food; for Jesus hungered, and they shall be filled. Blessed are those who mourn, if they mourn not only for their afflictions, but for their sins, and for the sins they see around them; for on this day, Jesus mourned for our sins; on this day He was made sin for us, who knew no sin, and they shall be comforted. Blessed are those who are ashamed of themselves, and hate themselves, and humble themselves before God this day; for on this day Jesus humbled Himself for us; and they shall be exalted. Blessed are the forsaken and the despised.— Did not all men forsake Jesus this day, in His hour of need? and why not thee, too, thou poor deserted one? Shall the disciple be above his Master? No; every one that is perfect, must be like his master. The deeper, the bitterer your loneliness, the more are you like Him, who cried upon the cross, 'My God, my God, why hast Thou forsaken Me?' He knows what that grief, too, is like.

GOOD FRIDAY.

He feels for thee, at least. Though all forsake thee, He is with thee still; and if he be with thee, what matter who has left thee for a while? Ay, blessed are those that weep now, for they shall laugh. It is those whom the Lord loveth that He chasteneth. And because He loves the poor, He brings them low. All things are blessed now, but sin; for all things, excepting sin, are redeemed by the life and death of the Son of God. Blessed are wisdom and courage, joy, and health, and beauty, love and marriage, childhood and manhood, corn and wine, fruits and flowers, for Christ redeemed them by His life. And blessed, too, are tears and shame, blessed are weakness and ugliness, blessed are agony and sickness, blessed the sad remembrance of our sins, and a broken heart, and a repentant spirit. Blessed is death, and blest the unknown realms, where souls await the resurrection day, for Christ redeemed them by His death. Blessed are all things, weak, as well as strong. Blessed are all days, dark, as well as bright, for all are His, and He is ours; and all are ours, and we are His, for ever.

Therefore sigh on, ye sad ones, and rejoice in your own sadness; ache on, ye suffering ones, and rejoice in your own sorrows. Rejoice that you are made free of the holy brotherhood of mourners, that you may claim your place, too, if you will, among the noble army of martyrs. Rejoice that you are counted worthy of a fellowship in the sufferings of the Son of God. Rejoice and trust on, for after sorrow shall come joy. Trust on; for in man's weakness God's strength shall be made perfect. Trust on, for death is the gate of life. Endure on to the end, and possess your souls in patience for a little while, and that, perhaps, a very little while. Death comes swiftly; and more swiftly still, perhaps, the day of the Lord. The deeper the sorrow, the nearer the salvation :—

> The night is darkest before the dawn;
> When the pain is sorest the child is born;
> And the day of the Lord at hand.

Ay, if the worst should come; if neither the laws of your country nor the benevolence of the righteous were strong enough to defend you; if one charitable plan after another were to fail; if the labour-market were getting fuller and fuller, and poverty were spreading wider and wider, and crime and misery were breeding faster and still faster every year than education and religion ; all hope for the poor seemed gone and lost, and they were ready to believe the men who tell them that the land is over-peopled—that there are too many of us, too many industrious hands, too many cunning brains, too many immortal souls, too many of God's children upon God's earth, which God the

Father made, and God the Son redeemed, and God the Holy Spirit teaches: then the Lord, the Prince of sufferers, He who knows your every grief, and weeps with you tear for tear, He would come out of His place to smite the haughty ones, and confound the cunning ones, and silence the loud ones, and empty the full ones; to judge with righteousness for the meek of the earth, to hearken to the prayer of the poor, whose heart He has been preparing, and to help the fatherless and needy to their right, that the man of the world may be no more exalted against them.

In that day men will find out a wonder and a miracle. They will see many that are first last, and many that are last first. They will find that there were poor who were the richest after all; and simple who were wisest, and gentle who were bravest, and weak who were strongest; that God's ways are not as men's ways, nor God's thoughts as men's thoughts? Alas, who shall stand when God does this? At least He who will do it is Jesus, who loved us to the death; boundless love and gentleness, boundless generosity and pity; who was tempted even as we are, who has felt our every weakness. In that thought is utter comfort, that our Judge will be He who died and rose again, and is praying for us even now, to His Father and our Father. Therefore fear not, gentle souls, patient souls, pure consciences and tender hearts. Fear not, you who are empty and hungry, who walk in darkness and see no light; for though He fulfil once more, as He has again and again, the awful prophecy before the text; though He tread down the people in His anger, and make them drunk in His fury, and bring their strength to the earth; though kings with their armies may flee, and the stars which light the earth may fall, and there be great tribulation, wars, and rumours of wars, and on earth distress of nations with perplexity—yet it is when the day of His vengeance is at hand, that the year of His redeemed is come. And when they see all these things, let them rejoice and lift up their heads, for their redemption draweth nigh.

Do you ask how I know this? Do you ask for a sign, for a token that these my words are true? I know that they are true. But, as for tokens, I will give you but this one, the sign of that bread and that wine. When the Lord shall have delivered His people out of all their sorrows, they shall eat of that bread and drink of that wine, one and all, in the kingdom of God.

VIII.

EASTER-DAY.

COLOSSIANS. iii. 1.

If ye then be risen with Christ, seek those things which are above, where Christ sitteth on the right hand of God.

I KNOW no better way of preaching to you the gospel of Easter, the good news which this day brings to all men, year after year, than by trying to explain to you the Epistle appointed for this day, which we have just read.

It begins, 'If ye then be risen with Christ.' Now that does not mean that St. Paul had any doubt whether the Colossians to whom he was speaking, were risen with Christ or not. He does not mean, 'I am not sure whether you are risen or not; but perhaps you are not; but if you are, you ought to do such and such things.' He does not mean that. He was quite sure that these Colossians were risen with Christ. He had no doubt of it whatsoever. If you look at the chapter before, he says so. He tells them that they were buried with Christ in baptism, in which also they were risen with Christ, through faith of the operation of God, who has raised Him from the dead.

Now what reason had St. Paul to believe that these Colossians were risen with Jesus Christ? Because they had given up sin, and were leading holy lives? That cannot be. The Epistle for this day says the very opposite. It does not say, 'You are risen, because you have left off sinning.' It says, 'You must leave off sinning, because you are risen.' Was it then on account of any experiences, or inward feeling of theirs? Not at all. He says that these Colossians had been baptized, and that they had believed in God's work of raising Jesus Christ from the dead, and that therefore they were risen with Christ. In one word, they had believed the message of Easter-day, and therefore they shared in the blessings of Easter-day; as it is written in another place, 'If thou shalt confess with thy mouth the Lord Jesus Christ, and believe in thy heart that God has raised Him from the dead, thou shalt be saved.'

Now these seem very wide words, too wide to please most people. But there are wider words still in St. Paul's epistles. He tells us again and again that God's mercy is a free gift; that He has made to us a free present of His Son Jesus Christ. That He has taken away the effect of all men's sin; and more than that, that men are God's children; that they have a right to believe that they are so, because they are so. For, He says,

EASTER-DAY.

the free gift of Jesus Christ is not like Adam's offence. It is not less than it, narrower than it, as some folks say. It is not that by Adam's sin all became sinners, and by Jesus Christ's salvation an elect few out of them shall be made righteous. If you will think a moment, you will see that it cannot be so. For Jesus Christ conquered sin and death and the devil. But if, as some think, sin and death and the devil have destroyed and sent to hell by far the greater part of mankind, then they have conquered Christ, and not Christ them. Mankind belonged to Christ at first. Sin and death and the devil came in and ruined them, and then Christ came to redeem them; but if all that He has been able to do is to redeem one out of a thousand, or, even nine out of ten, of them, then the devil has had the best of the battle. He, and not Christ, is the conqueror. If a thief steals all the sheep on your farm, and all that you can get back from him is a part of the whole flock, which has had the best of it, you or the thief? If Christ's redemption is meant for only a few, or even a great many elect souls out of all the millions of mankind, which has had the best of it, Christ, the master of the sheep, or the devil, the robber and destroyer of them? Be sure, my friends, Christ is stronger than that; His love is deeper than that; His redemption is wider than that. How strong, how deep, how wide it is, we never shall know. St. Paul tells us that we never shall know, for it is boundless: but that we shall go on knowing more and more of its vastness for ever, finding it deeper, wider, loftier than our most glorious dreams could ever picture it. But this, he says, we do know, that we have gained more than Adam lost. For if by one man's offence many were made sinners, much more shall they who receive abundance of grace and of the gift of righteousness reign in life by one, even Jesus Christ. For, he says, where sin abounded, God's grace and free gift has much more abounded. Therefore, as by the offence of one, judgment came upon all men to condemnation, even so by the righteousness of one the free gift came upon all men to justification of life. Upon all men, you see. There can be no doubt about it. Upon you and me, and foreigners, and gipsies, and heathens, and thieves, and harlots—upon all mankind, let them be as bad or as good, as young or as old, as they may, the free gift of God has come to justification of life; they are justified, pardoned, and beloved in the sight of Almighty God; they have a right and a share to a new life; a different sort of life from what they are inclined to lead, and do lead, by nature—to a life which death cannot take away, a life which may grow, and strengthen, and widen, and blossom, and bear fruit for ever and ever. They have a share in Christ's resurrection, in the blessing of Easter-day. They have a share in Christ, every one of them, whether they claim that share or not. How far they will be punished for not claiming it, is a very different matter, of which we know nothing whatsoever. And how far the heathen who have never heard of Christ, or of their share in Him, will be punished, we know not—we are not meant to know. But we know that to their own Master they stand or fall, and that their Master is our Master too, and that He is a just Master, and requires little of him to whom He gives little;— a just and merciful Master, who loved this sinful world enough to come down and die for it, while mankind were all rebels and sinners, and has gone on taking care of it, and improving it, in spite of all its sin and rebellion ever since, and that is enough for us.

St. Paul knew no more. It was a mystery, he says, a wonderful and unfathomable matter, which had been hidden since the foundation of the world, of which he himself says that he saw only through a glass darkly; and we cannot expect to have clearer eyes than he. But this he seems to have seen, that the Lord, when He rose again, bought a blessing even for the dumb beasts and the earth on which we live. For he says, the whole creation is now groaning in the pangs of labour, being about to bring forth something ; and the whole creation will rise again ; how, and when, and into what new state, we cannot tell. But St. Paul seems to say that when the Lord shall destroy death, the last of His enemies, then the whole creation shall be renewed, and bring forth another earth, nobler, and more beautiful than this one, free from death, and sin, and sorrow, and redeemed into the glorious liberty of the children of God.

But this, on the other hand, St. Paul did see most clearly, and preached it to all to whom he spoke, that the ground and reason of this great and glorious mystery was the thing which happened on the first Easter-day, namely, the Lord Jesus rising from the dead. About that, at least, there was no doubt at all in his mind. We may see it by the Easter anthem, which we read this morning, taken out of the fifteenth chapter of his first epistle to the Corinthians!—

'Christ is risen from the dead, and become the first fruits of them that slept.

'For since by man came death, by man came also the resurrection of the dead.

'For as in Adam all die, even so in Christ shall all be made alive.'

Now he is not talking here merely of the rising again of our bodies at the last day. That was in his mind only the end, and outcome, and fruit, and perfecting, of men's rising from the dead in this life. For he tells these same Corinthians, and the Colossians, and others to whom he wrote, that life, the eternal life which would raise their bodies at the last day, was even then working in them.

Neither is he speaking only of a few believers. He says that, owing to the Lord's rising on this day, all shall be made alive—not merely all Christians, but all men. For he does not say, as in Adam all Christians die, but all men; and so he does not say, all Christians shall be made alive, but all men. For here, as in the sixth chapter of Romans, he is trying to make us understand the likeness between Adam and Jesus Christ, whom he calls the new Adam. The first Adam, he says, was only a living soul, as the savages and heathens are; but the second Adam, the Lord from heaven, the true pattern of men, is a quickening, life-giving spirit, to give eternal life to every human being who will accept His offer, and claim his share and right as a true man, after the likeness of the new Adam, Jesus Christ.

We then, every one of us who is here to-day, have a right to believe that we have a share in Christ's eternal life: that our original sin, that is, the sinfulness which we inherited from our forefathers, is all forgiven and forgotten, and that mankind is now redeemed, and belongs to the second Adam, the true and original head and pattern of man, Jesus Christ, in whom was no sin; and that because mankind belongs to Him, God is well pleased with them, and reconciled to them, and looks on them not as a guilty, but as a pardoned and beloved race of beings.

And we have a right to believe also, that because all power is given to Christ in heaven and earth, there is given to Him the power of making men what they ought to be—like His own blessed, and glorious, and perfect self. Ask Him, and you shall receive; knock at the gate of His treasure-house, and it shall be opened. Seek those things that are above, and you shall find them. You shall find old bad habits die out in you, new good habits spring up in you; old meannesses become weaker, new nobleness and manfulness become stronger; the old, selfish, covetous, savage, cunning, cowardly, brutal Adam dying out, the new, loving, brotherly, civilized, wise, brave, manful Adam growing up in you, day by day, to perfection, till you are changed from grace to grace, and glory to glory, into the likeness of the Lord of men.

'These are great promises,' you may say, 'glorious promises; but what proof have you that they belong to us? They sound too good to be true; too great for such poor creatures as we are;

give us but some proof that we have a right to them ; give us but a pledge from Jesus Christ ; give us but a sign, an assurance from God, and we may believe you then."

My friends, I am certain—and the longer I live I am the more certain—that there is no argument, no pledge, no sign, no assurance, like the bread and the wine upon that table. Assurances in our own hearts and souls are good, but we may be mistaken about them ; for, after all, they are our own thoughts, notions in our own souls, these inward experiences and assurances ; delightful and comforting as they are at times, yet we cannot trust them—we cannot trust our own hearts, they are deceitful above all things, who can know them? Yes : our own hearts may tell us lies ; they may make us fancy that we are pleasing God, when we are doing the things most hateful to him. They have made thousands fancy so already. They may make us fancy we are right in God's sight, when we are utterly wrong. They have made thousands fancy so already. These hearts of ours may make us fancy that we have spiritual life in us ; that we are in a state higher and nobler than the sinners round us, when all the while our spirits are dead within us. They made the Pharisees of old fancy that their souls were alive, and pure, and religious, when they were dead and damned within them ;

and they may make us fancy so too. No: we cannot trust our hearts and inward feelings; but that bread, that wine, we can trust. Our inward feelings are a sign from man: that bread and wine are a sign from God. Our inward feelings may tell us what we feel toward God: that bread, that wine, tell us something ten thousand times more important; they tell us what God feels toward us. And God must love us before we can love Him; God must pardon us before we can have mercy on ourselves; God must come to us, and take hold of us, before we can cling to Him; God must change us, before we can become right; God must give us eternal life in our hearts before we can feel and enjoy that new life in us. Then that bread, that wine say that God has done all that for us already; they say, 'God does love you; God has pardoned you; God has has come to you; God is ready and willing to change and convert you; God has given you eternal life: and this love, this mercy, this coming to find you out while you are wandering in sin, this change, this eternal life, are all in His Son Jesus Christ; and that bread, that wine, are the signs of it. It is for the sake of Jesus' blood that God has pardoned you, and that cup is the new covenant in His blood. Come and drink, and claim your pardon. It is simply because Jesus Christ was man, and you, too, are men and women, wearing the flesh and blood which Christ wore; eating and drinking as Christ ate and drank, and not for any works or faith of your own, that God loves you, and has come to you, and called you into His family. This is the Gospel, the good news of Christ's free grace, and pardon, and salvation; and that bread, that wine, the common food of all men, not merely of the rich, or the wise, or the pious, but of saints and penitents, rich and poor, Christians and heathens, alike—that plain, common, every-day bread and wine—are the signs of it. Come and take the signs, and claim your share in God's love, in God's family. And it is in Jesus Christ, too, that you have eternal life. It is because you belong to Jesus Christ, to mankind, of which He is the head and king, that God will change you, strengthen your soul to rise above your sins, raise you up daily more and more out of spiritual death, out of brutishness, and selfishness, and ignorance, and malice, into an eternal life of wisdom, and love, and courage, and mercifulness, and patience, and obedience; a life which shall continue through death, and beyond death, and raise you up again for ever at the last day, because you belong to Christ's body, and have been fed with Christ's eternal life. And that bread, that wine, are the signs of it. 'Take, eat,' said Jesus, 'this is my body; drink, this is my blood.' Those are the signs that God has given you eternal life, and that this life is in His Son. What better sign would you have? There is no mistaking their message; they can tell you no lies. And they can, and will, bring your own Gospel-blessings to your mind, as nothing else can. They will make you feel, as nothing else can, that you are the beloved children of God, heirs of all that your King and Head has bought for you, when He died, and rose again upon this day. He gave you the Lord's Supper for a sign. Do you think that He did not know best what the best sign would be? He said, 'Do this in remembrance of me?' Do you think that He did not know better than you, and me, and all men, that if you did do it, it would put you in remembrance of Him?

Oh! come to His table, this day of all days in the year; and claim there your share in His body and His blood, to feed the everlasting life in you; which, though you see it not now, though you feel it not now, will surely, if you keep it alive in you by daily faith, and daily repentance, and daily prayer, and daily obedience, raise you up, body and soul, to reign with Him for ever at the last day.

IX.

THE COMFORTER.

FOURTH SUNDAY AFTER EASTER.

JOHN xvi. 7.

If I go not away, the Comforter will not come unto you; but if I depart, I will send Him unto you.

WE are now coming near to two great days, Ascension-day, and Whit-Sunday, which our forefathers have appointed, year by year, to put us continually in mind of two great works, which the Lord worked out for us, His most unworthy subjects, and still unworthier brothers.

On Ascension-day He ascended up into Heaven, and received gifts for men, even for His enemies, that the Lord God might dwell among them; and on Whit-Sunday, He sent down those gifts. The Spirit of God came down to dwell in the hearts of men, to be the right of every one who asks for it, white or black, young or old, rich or poor, and never to leave this earth as long as there is a human being on it. And because we are coming near to these two great days, the Prayer-book, in the Collects, Epistles, and Gospels, tries to put us in mind of those days, and to make us ready to ask for the blessings of which they are the yearly signs and witnesses. The Gospel for last Sunday told us how the Lord told His disciples just before His death, that for a little while they should not see Him; and again a little while and they should see Him, because He was going to the Father, and that they should have great sorrow, but that their sorrow should be turned into joy. And the Gospel for to-day goes further still, and tells us why He was going away—that He might send to them the Comforter, His Holy Spirit, and that it was expedient—good for them, that He should go away; for that if He did not, the Comforter would not come to them. Now, in these words, I do not doubt He was speaking of Ascension-day, and of Whit-Sunday; and therefore it is that these Gospels have been chosen to be read before Ascension-day and Whit-Sunday; and in proportion as we attend to these Gospels, and take in the meaning of them, and act accordingly, Ascension-day and Whit-Sunday will be a blessing and a profit to us; and in proportion as we neglect them, or forget them, Ascension-day and Whit-Sunday will be witnesses against our souls at the day of judgment, that the Lord Himself condescended to buy for us with His own blood, blessings unspeakable, and offer them freely unto us, in spite of all our sins, and yet we would have none of them, but preferred our own will to God's will, and the little which we thought we could get for ourselves to the unspeakable treasures which God had promised to give us, and turned away from the blessings of His kingdom, to our own foolish pleasure and covetousness, like 'the dog to his vomit, and the sow that was washed to her wallowing in the mire.'

I said that God had promised to us an unspeakable treasure: and so He has; a treasure that will make the poorest and weakest man among us, richer than if he had all the wealth gathered from all the nations of the world, which every one is admiring now in that Great Exhibition in London, and stronger than if he had all the wisdom which produced that wealth. Let us see now what it is that God has promised us—and then those to whom God has given ears to hear, and hearts to understand, will see that large as my words may sound, they are no larger than the truth.

Christ said, that if He went away, He would send down the Comforter, the Holy Spirit of God. The Nicene Creed says, that the Holy Spirit of God is the Lord and Giver of life; and so He is. He gives life to the earth, to the trees, to the flowers, to the dumb animals, to the bodies and minds of men; all life, all growth, all health, all strength, all beauty, all order, all help and assistance of one thing by another, which you see in the world around you, comes from Him. He is the Lord and Giver of life; in Him, the earth, the sun and stars, all live and move and have their being. He is not them, or a part of them, but He gives life to them. But to men he is more than that—for we men ourselves are more than that, and need more. We have immortal spirits in us— a reason, a conscience, and a will; strange rights and duties, strange hopes and fears, of which the beasts and the plants know nothing. We have hearts in us which can love, and feel, and sorrow, and be weak, and sinful, and mistaken; and therefore we want a Comforter. And the Lord and Giver of life has promised to be our Comforter; and the Father and the Son, from both of whom He proceeds, have promised to send Him to us, to strengthen and comfort us, and give our spirits life and health, and knit us together to each other, and to God, in one common bond of love and fellow-feeling, even as He the Spirit knits together the Father and the Son.

I said that we want a Comforter. If we consider what that word Comforter means, we shall see that we do want a Comforter, and that the only Comforter which can satisfy us for ever and ever, must be He, the very Spirit of God, the Lord and Giver of life.

Now Comforter means one who gives comfort; so the meaning of it will depend upon what comfort means. Our word comfort, comes from two old Latin words, which mean *with* and *to strengthen*. And, therefore, a Comforter means any one who is with us to strengthen us, and do for us what we could not do for ourselves. You will see that this is the proper meaning of the word, when you remember what bodily things we call comforts. You say that a person is comfortable, or lives in comfort, if he has a comfortable income, a comfortable house, comfortable clothes, comfortable food, and so on. Now all these things, his money, his house, his clothes, his food, are not himself. They make him stronger and more at ease. They make his life more pleasant to him. But they are not *him;* they are round him, with him, to strengthen him. So with a person's mind and feelings; when a man is in sorrow and trouble, he cannot comfort himself. His friends must come to him and comfort him; talk to him, advise him, show their kind feeling towards him, and in short, be with him to strengthen him in his afflictions. And if we require comfort for our bodies, and for our minds, my friends, how much more do we for our spirits—our souls, as we call them! How weak, and ignorant, and self-willed, and perplexed, and sinful they are—surely our souls require a comforter far more than our bodies or our minds do! And to comfort our spirits, we require a spirit; for we cannot see our own spirits, our own souls, as we can our bodies. We cannot even tell by our feelings what state they are in. We may deceive ourselves, and we do deceive ourselves, again and again, and fancy that our souls are strong when they are weak—that they are simple and truthful when they are full of deceit and falsehood—that they are loving God when they are only loving themselves—that they are doing God's will when they are only doing their own selfish and perverse wills. No man can take care of his own spirit, much less give his own spirit life; 'no man can quicken his own soul,' says David, that is, no man can give his own soul life. And therefore we must have some one beyond ourselves to give life to our spirits. We must have some one to teach us the things that we could never find out for ourselves, some one who will put into our hearts the good desires that could never come of themselves. We must have some one who can change these wills of ours, and make them love what they hate by nature, and make them hate what they love by nature. For by nature we are selfish. By nature we are inclined to love ourselves rather than any one else ; to take care of ourselves, rather than any one else. By nature we are inclined to follow our own will, rather than God's will, to do our own pleasure, rather than follow God's commandments, and therefore by nature our spirits are dead ; for selfishness and self-will are *spiritual death*. Spiritual life is love, pity, patience, courage, honesty, truth, justice, humbleness, industry, self-sacrifice, obedience to God, and therefore to those whom God sends to teach and guide us. *That* is spiritual life. That is the life of Jesus Christ ; His character, His conduct, was like that—to love, to help, to pity, all around—to give up Himself even to death—to do His Father's will and not His own. That was His life. Because He was the Son of God He did it. In proportion as we live like Him, we shall be living like sons of God. In proportion as we live like Jesus Christ, the Son of God, our spirits will be alive. For he that hath Jesus Christ the Son of God in him, hath life, and he that hath not the Son of God, hath not life, says St. John. But who can raise us from the death of sin and selfishness, to the life of righteousness and love? Who can change us into the likeness of Jesus Christ? Who can even show us what Jesus Christ's likeness is, and take the things of Christ and show them to us ; so that by seeing what He was, we may see what we should be? And who, if we have this life in us, will keep it alive in us, and be with us to strengthen us? Who will give us strength to force the foul and fierce and false thoughts out of our mind, and say, 'Get thee behind me, Satan?' Who will give our spirits life? and who will strengthen that life in us?

Can we do it for ourselves? Oh! my friends, I pity the man who is so blind and ignorant, who knows so little of himself, upon whom the lessons which his own mistakes, and sins, and failings, should have taught him, have been so wasted, that he fancies that he can teach and guide himself without any help, and that he can raise his own soul to life, or keep it alive without assistance. Can his body do without its comforts? Then how can his spirit? If he left his house, and threw away his clothes, and refused all help from his fellow-men, and went and lived in the woods like a wild beast, we should call him a madman, because he refused the help and comfort to his body which God has made necessary for him. But just as great a madman is he who refuses the help and the strengthening which God has made necessary for his spirit—just as great a madman is he who fancies that his soul is any more able than his body is, to live without continual help. It is just because man is nobler than the beast that he requires help. The fox in the wood needs no house, no fire; he needs no friends; he needs no comforts, and no comforters, because he is a beast— because he is meant to live and die selfish and alone; therefore God has provided him in himself with all things necessary to keep the poor brute selfish life in him for a few short years. But just because man is nobler than that; just because man is not intended to live selfish and alone; just because his body, and his mind, and his spirit, are beautifully and delicately made, and intended for all sorts of wonderful purposes, therefore God has appointed that from the moment he is born to all eternity he cannot live alone; he cannot support himself; he stands in continual need of the assistance of all around him, for body, and soul, and spirit; he needs clothes, which other men must make; houses, which other men must build; food, which other men must produce; he has to get his livelihood by working for others, while others get their livelihood in return by working for him. As a child he needs his parents to be his comforters, to take care of him in body and mind. As he grows up he needs the care of others; he cannot exist a day without his fellow-men: he requires schoolmasters to educate him; books and masters to teach him his trade; and when he has learnt it, and settled himself in life, he requires laws made by other men, perhaps by men who died hundreds of years before he was born, to secure to him his rights and property, to secure to him comforts, and to make him feel comfortable in his station; he needs friends and a family to comfort him in sorrow and in joy, to do for him the thousand things which he cannot do for himself. In proportion as he is alone and friendless, he is pitiable and miserable, let him be as rich as Solomon himself. From the moment, I say, he is born, he needs continual comforts and comforters for his body, and mind, and heart. And then he fancies that, though his body and his mind cannot exist safely, or grow up healthily, without the continual care and comforting of his fellow-men, that yet his *soul*, the part of him which is at once the most important and the most in danger; the part of him of which he knows least; the part of him which he understands least; the part of him of which his body and mind cannot take care, because it has to take care of them, can live, and grow, and prosper, without any help whatsoever!

And if we cannot strengthen our own souls, no man can strengthen them for us. No man can raise our bodies to life, much less can he raise our souls. The physician himself cannot cure the sicknesses of our bodies; he can only give us fit medicines, and leave them to cure us by certain laws of nature, which he did not make, and which he cannot alter. And though the physician can, by much learning, understand men's bodies somewhat, who can understand men's souls? We cannot understand our own souls; we do not know what they are, how they live; whence they come, or whither they go. We cannot cure them ourselves, much less can any one cure them for us. The only one who can cure our souls is He that made our souls; the only one who can give life to our souls is He who gives life to everything. The only one who can cure, and strengthen, and comfort our spirits, is He who understands our spirits, because He himself is the Spirit of all spirits, the Spirit who searcheth all things, even the deep things of God; because He is the Spirit of God the Father, who made all heaven and earth, and of Jesus Christ the Son, who understands the heart of man, who can be touched with the feelings of our infirmities, and hath been tempted in all things, just as we are, yet without sin.

He is the Comforter which God has promised to our spirits, the only Comforter who can strengthen our spirits; and if we have Him with us, if He is strengthening us, if He is leading us, if He is abiding with us, if He is changing us day by day, more and more, into the likeness of Jesus Christ, are we not, as I said at the beginning of my sermon, richer than if we possessed all the land of England, stronger than if we had all the armies of the world at our command? For what is more precious than —God Himself? What is stronger than—God Himself? The poorest man in whom God's Spirit dwells, is greater than the greatest king in whom God's Spirit does not dwell. And so he will find in the day that he dies. Then where will riches be, and power? The rich man will take none of them away with him when he dieth, neither shall his pomp follow him. Naked came he into this world, and naked shall he return out of it, to go as he came, and carry with him none of the comforts which he thought in this life the only ones worth having. But the Spirit of God remains with us for ever; that treasure a man shall carry out of this world with him, and keep to all eternity. That friend will never forsake him, for He is the Spirit of Love, which abideth for ever. That Comforter will never grow weak, for He is Himself The very eternal Lord and Giver of life; and the soul that is possessed by Him must live, must grow, must become nobler, purer, freer, stronger, more loving, for ever and ever, as the eternities roll by. That is what He will give you, my friends; that is His treasure; that is the Spirit-life, the true and everlasting life, which flows from Him, as the stream flows from the fountain-head.

X.

WHIT-SUNDAY.

GALATIANS V. 22, 23.

The fruit of the Spirit is love, joy, peace, longsuffering, gentleness, goodness, faith, meekness, temperance—against such there is no law.

IN all countries, and in all ages, the world has been full of complaints of Law and Government. And one hears the same complaints in England now. You hear complaints that the laws favour one party and one rank more than another, that they are expensive, and harsh, and unfair, and what not?—But I think, my friends, that for us, and especially on this Whit-Sunday, it will be much wiser, instead of complaining of the laws, to complain of ourselves, for needing those laws. For what is it that makes laws necessary at all, except man's sinfulness? Adam required no laws in the garden of Eden. We should require no laws if we were what we ought to be—what God has offered to make us. We may see this by looking at the laws themselves, and considering the purposes for which they were made. We shall then see, that like Moses' Laws of old, the greater part of them have been added because of transgressions.—In plain English—to prevent men from doing things which they ought not to do, and which, if they were in a right state of mind, they would not do. How many laws are passed, simply to prevent one man, or one class, from oppressing or ill-using some other man or class? What a vast number of them are passed simply to protect property, or to protect the weak from the cruel, the ignorant from the cunning! It is plain that if there was no cruelty, no cunning, no dishonesty, these laws, at all events, would not be needed. Again, one of the great complaints against the laws and the government, is, that they are so expensive, that rates and taxes are heavy burdens—and doubtless they are: but what makes them necessary except men's sin? If the poor were more justly and mercifully treated, and if they in their turn were more thrifty and provident, there would be no need of the expenses of poor rates. If there was no love of war and plunder, there would be no need of the expense of an army. If there was no crime, there would be no need of the expense of police and prisons. The thing is so simple and self-evident, that it seems almost childish to mention it. And yet, my friends, we forget it daily. We complain of the laws and their harshness, of taxes and their expensiveness, and we forget all the while that it is our own selfishness and sinfulness which brings this expense upon us, which makes it necessary for the law to interfere and protect us against others, and others against us. And while we are complaining of the government for not doing its work somewhat more cheaply, we are forgetting that if we chose, we might leave government very little work to do—that every man if he chose, might be his own law-maker, and his own police—that every man if he will, may lead a life 'against which there is no law.'

I say again, that it is our own fault, the fault of our sinfulness, that laws are necessary for us. In proportion as we are what Scripture calls 'natural men,' that is, savage, selfish, divided from each other, and struggling against each other, each for his own interest; as long as we are not renewed and changed into new men, so long will laws, heavy, severe, and burdensome, be necessary for us. Without them we should be torments to ourselves, to our neighbours, to our country. But these laws are only necessary as long as we are full of selfishness and ungodliness. The moment we yield ourselves up to God's law, man's laws are ready enough to leave us alone. Take, for instance, a common example; as long as any one is a faithful husband and a good father, the law does not interfere with his conduct towards his wife and children. But it is when he is unfaithful to them, when he ill-treats them, or deserts them, that the law interferes with its "Thou shalt not," and compels him to behave, against his will, in the way in which he ought to have behaved of his own will. It was free to the man to have done his duty by his family, without the law—the moment he neglects his duty, he becomes amenable to it.

But the law can only force a man's actions: it cannot change his heart. In the instance which I have been just mentioning, the law can say to a man 'You shall not ill-treat your family; you shall not leave them to starve.' But the law cannot say to him 'You shall love your family.' The law can only command from a man outward obedience; the obedience of the heart it cannot enforce. The law may make a man do his duty, it cannot make a man *love* his duty. And therefore laws will never set the world right. They can punish persons after the wrong is done, and that not certainly nor always: but they cannot certainly prevent the wrongs being done. The law can punish a man for stealing: and yet, as we see daily, men steal in the face of punishment. Or even if the law, by its severity, makes persons afraid to commit certain particular crimes, yet still as long as the sinful heart is left in them unchanged, the sin which is checked in one direction is sure to break out in another. Sin, like every other disease, is sure, when it is driven onwards, to break out at a fresh point, or fester within in some still more deadly, because more hidden and unsuspected, shape. The man who dare not be an open sinner for fear of the law, can be a hypocrite in spite of it. The man who dare not steal for fear of the law, can cheat in spite of it. The selfish man will find fresh ways of being selfish, the tyrannical man of being tyrannical, however closely the law may watch him. He will discover some means of evading it; and thus the law, after all, though it may keep down crime, multiplies sin; and by the law, as St. Paul says, is the knowledge of sin.

What then will do that for this poor world which the law cannot do—which, as St. Paul tells us, not even the law of God given on Mount Sinai, holy, just, good as it was, could do, because no law can give life? What will give men a new heart and a new spirit, which shall love its duty and do it willingly, and not by compulsion, everywhere and always, and not merely just as far as it is commanded? The text tells us that there is a Spirit, the fruit of which is love, joy, peace, long-suffering, gentleness, goodness, faith, meekness, temperance; a character such as no laws can give to a man, and which no law dare punish in a man. Look at this character as St. Paul sets it forth—and then think what need would there be of all these burdensome and expensive laws, if all men were but full of the fruits of that Spirit which St. Paul describes?

I know what answer will be ready, in some of your minds at least, to all this. You will be ready to reply, almost angrily, 'Of course if every one was perfect, we should need no laws: but people are not perfect, and you cannot expect them to be.' My friends, whether or not *we* expect baptized people, living in a Christian country, to be perfect, God expects them to be perfect; for He has said, by the mouth of His Son, our Lord Jesus Christ, 'Be ye therefore perfect, as our Father which is in heaven is perfect.' And He has told us what being perfect is like; you may read it for yourselves in His sermon on the Mount; and you may see also that what He commands us to do in that sermon, from the beginning to the end, is the exact opposite and contrary of the ways and rules of this world, which, as I have shown, make burdensome laws necessary to prevent our devouring each other. Now, do you think that God would have told us to be perfect, if He knew that it was impossible for us? Do you think that He, the God of truth, would have spoken such a cruel mockery against poor sinful creatures like us, as to command us a duty without giving us the means of fulfilling it? Do you think that He did not know ten thousand times better than I, what I have been just telling you, that laws could not change men's hearts and wills; that commanding a man to love and like a thing will not make him love and like it; that a man's heart and spirit must be changed in him from within, and not merely laws and commandments laid on him from without? Then why has He commanded us to love each other, ay, to love our enemies, to bless those who curse us, to pray for those who use us spitefully? Do you think the Lord meant to make hypocrites of us; to tell us to go about, as some who call themselves religious do go about, with their lips full of meek, and humble, and simple, and loving words, while their hearts are full of pride, and spite, and cunning, and hate, and selfishness, which are all the more deadly for being kept in and plastered over by a smooth outside? God forbid! He tells us to love each other, only because He has promised us the spirit of love. He tells us to be humble, because He can make us humble-hearted. He tells us to be honest, because He can make us love and delight in honesty. He tells us to refrain ourselves from foul thoughts as well as from foul actions, because He can take the foul heart out of us, and give us instead the spirit of purity and holiness. He tells us to lead new lives after the new pattern of Himself, because He can give us new hearts and a new spring of life within us; in short, He bids us behave as sons of God should behave, because, as He said Himself, 'If we, being evil, know how to give our children what is good for them, much more will our heavenly Father give His Holy Spirit to those who ask Him.' If you would be perfect, ask your Father in heaven to make you perfect. If you feel that your heart is wrong, ask Him to give you a new and a right heart. If you feel yourselves—as you are, whether you feel it or not—too weak, too ignorant, too selfish, to guide yourselves, ask Him to send His Spirit to guide you; ask for the Spirit from which comes all love, all light, all wisdom, all strength of mind. Ask for that Spirit, and you *shall* receive it; seek for it, and you shall find it; knock at the gate of your Father's treasure-house, and it shall be surely opened to you.

But some of you, perhaps, are saying to yourselves, 'How will my being changed and renewed by the Spirit of God, render the laws less burdensome, while the crime and sin around me remain unchanged? It is others who want to be improved as much, and perhaps more than I do.' It may be so, my friends; or again, it may not; those

WHIT-SUNDAY. 119

they do, may be the very persons who need it really the most; those who say they see, may be only proving their blindness by so saying; those who fancy that their souls are rich, and are full of all knowledge, and understand the whole Bible, and want no further teaching, may be, as they were in St. John's time, just the ones who are wretched, and miserable, and poor, and blind, and naked, in soul, and do not know it. But at all events, if you think others need to be changed by God's Spirit, *pray* that God's Spirit may change them. For believe me, unless you pray for God's Spirit for each other, ay, for the whole world, there is no use asking for yourselves. This, I believe, is one of the reasons, perhaps the chief reason, why the fruits of God's Spirit are so little seen among us in these days; why our Christianity is become more and more dead, and hollow, and barren, while expensive and intricate laws and taxes are becoming more and more necessary every year; because our religion has become so selfish, because we have been praying for God's Spirit too little for each other. Our prayers have become too selfish. We have been looking for God's Spirit not so much as a means to enable us to do good to others, but as some sort of mysterious charm which was to keep us ourselves from the punishment of our sins in the next life, or give us a higher place in heaven; and, therefore, St. James's words have been fulfilled to us, even in our very prayers for God's Spirit, "Ye ask and have not, because ye ask amiss, to consume it upon your lusts,"—to save our selfish souls from the pains of hell; to give our selfish souls selfish pleasures and selfish glorification in the world to come: but not to spread God's kingdom upon earth, not to make us live on earth such lives as Christ lived; a life of love and self-sacrifice, and continual labour for the souls of others. Therefore it is, that God's Spirit is not poured out upon us in these days; for God's Spirit is the spirit of love and brotherhood, which delivers a man from his selfishness; and if we do not desire to be delivered from our selfishness, we do not desire the Spirit of God, and the Spirit of God will not be bestowed upon us. And no man desires to be delivered from his own selfishness, who in his very prayers, when he ought to be thinking least about himself alone, is thinking about himself most of all, and forgetting that he is the member of a family—that all mankind are his brethren—that he can claim nothing for himself to which every sinner around him has not an equal right—that nothing is necessary for him, which is not equally necessary for every one around him; that he has all the world besides himself to pray for, and that his prayers for himself will be heard only according as he prays for all the world beside. Baptism teaches us this,

WHITSUNDAY.

when it tells us that our old selfish nature is to be washed away, and a new character, after the pattern of Christ, is to live and grow up in us; that from the day we are baptized, to the day of our death, we should live not for ourselves, but for Jesus, in whom was no selfishness; when it teaches us that we are not only children of God, but members of Christ's Family, and heirs of God's kingdom, and therefore bound to make common cause with all other members of that Family, to live and labour for the common good of all our fellow-citizens in that kingdom. The Lord's prayer teaches us this, when He tells us to pray, not 'My Father,' but 'Our Father;' not 'my soul be saved,' but 'Thy kingdom come;' not 'give *me*,' but 'give *us* our daily bread;' not 'forgive *me*,' but 'forgive *us* our trespasses,' and that only as we forgive others; not 'lead *me* not,' but 'lead *us* not into temptation;' not 'deliver *me*,' but 'deliver *us* from evil.' After *that* manner the Lord told us to pray; and, in proportion as we pray in that manner, asking for nothing for ourselves which we do not ask for every one else in the whole world, just so far and no farther will God *hear* our prayers. He who asks for God's Spirit for himself only, and forgets that all the world need it as much as he, is not asking for God's Spirit at all, and does not know even what God's Spirit is. The mystery of

Pentecost, too, which came to pass on this day 1818 years ago, teaches us the same thing also. Those cloven tongues of fire, the tokens of God's Spirit, fell not upon one man, but upon many; not when they were apart from each other, but when they were together; and what were the fruits of that Spirit in the apostles? Did they remain within that upper room, each priding himself upon his own gifts, and trying merely to gain heaven for his own soul? If they had any such fancies, as they very likely had before the Spirit fell upon them, they had none such afterwards. The Spirit must have taken all such thoughts from them, and given them a new notion of what it was to be devout and holy: for instead of staying in that upper room, they went forth instantly into the public place to preach in foreign tongues to all the people. Instead of keeping themselves apart from each other in silence, and fancying, as some have done, and some do now, that they pleased God by being solitary, and melancholy, and selfish—what do we read? the fruit of God's Spirit was in them; that they and the three thousand souls who were added to them, on the first day of their preaching, 'were all together, and had all things common, and sold their possessions, and goods, and parted them to all men, as every man had need, and continuing daily with one accord in the temple, and breaking

WHIT-SUNDAY. 123

bread from house to house, did eat their bread in gladness and singleness of heart, praising God and having favour with all the people.' Those were the fruits of God's Spirit in *them*. Till we see more of that sort of life and society in England, we shall not be able to pride ourselves on having much of God's Spirit among us.

But above all, if anything will teach us that the strength of God's Spirit is not a strength which we must ask for for ourselves alone; that the blessings of God's kingdom are blessings which we cannot have in order to keep them to ourselves, but can only enjoy in as far as we share them with those around us; if any thing, I say, ought to teach us that lesson, it is the Sacrament of the Lord's Supper. Just consider a moment, my friends, what a strange thing it is, if we will think of it, that the Lord's Supper, the most solemn and sacred thing with which a man can have to do upon earth, is just a thing which he cannot transact for himself, or by himself. Not alone in secret, in his chamber, but, whether he will or not, in the company of others, not merely in the company of his own private friends, but in the company of any or every one, rich or poor, who chooses to kneel beside him; he goes with others, rich and poor alike, to the Lord's Table, and there the same bread, and the same wine, is shared among all by the same priest. If that means anything, it means this—that rich and poor alike draw life for their souls from the same well, not for themselves only, not apart from each other, but all in common, all together, because they are brothers, members of one family, as the leaves are members of the same tree; that as the same bread and the same wine are needed to nourish the bodies of all, the same spirit of God is needed to nourish the souls of all; and that we cannot have this spirit, except as members of a body, any more than a man's limb can have life when it is cut off and parted from him. This is the reason, and the only reason, why Protestant clergymen are forbidden, thank God! to give the Holy Sacrament of the Lord's Supper, to any one person singly. If a clergyman were to administer the Lord's Supper to himself in private, without any congregation to partake with him, it would not be the Lord's Supper, it would be nothing, and worse than nothing; it would be a sham and a mockery, and, I believe, a sin. I do not believe that Christ would be present, that God's Spirit would rest on that man. For our Lord says, that it is where two or three are gathered together in His name, that He is in the midst of them. And it was at a supper, at a feast, where all the Apostles were met together, that our Lord divided the bread amongst them, and told them to share the cup amongst themselves, just as a sign that they were all members of one body—that the welfare of each of them was bound up in the welfare of all the rest—that God's blessing did not rest upon each singly, but upon all together. And it is just because we have forgotten this, my friends—because we have forgotten that we are all brothers and sisters, children of one family, members of one body —because, in short, we have carried our selfishness into our very religion, and up to the altar of God, that we neglect the Lord's Supper as we do. People neglect the Lord's Supper because they either do not know or do not like that, of which the Lord's Supper is the token and warrant. It is not merely that they feel themselves unfit for the Lord's Supper, because they are not in love and charity with all men. Oh! my dear friends, do not some of your hearts tell you, that the reason why you stay away from the Lord's Supper is because you do not *wish* to be fit for the Lord's Supper—because you do not like to be in love and charity with all men—because you do not wish to be reminded that you are all equals in God's sight, all equally sinful, all equally pardoned—and to see people whom you dislike or despise, kneeling by your side, and partaking of the same bread and wine with you, as a token that God sees no difference between you and them; that God looks upon you all as brothers, however little brotherly love or fellow feeling there may be, alas! between you? Or, again, do not some of you stay away from the Lord's Supper, because you see no good in going? because it seems to make those who go no better than they were before? Shall I tell you the reason of that? Shall I tell you why, as is too true, too many do come to the Lord's Supper, and so far from being the better for it, seem only the worse? Because they come to it in selfishness. We have fallen into the same false and unscriptural way of looking at the Lord's Supper, into which the Papists have. People go to the Lord's Supper now-a-days too much to get some private good for their own souls, and it would not matter to many of them, I am afraid, if not another person in the parish received it, provided they can get, as they fancy, the same blessing from it. Thus they come to it in an utterly false and wrong temper of mind. Instead of coming as members of Christ's body, to get from Him life and strength, to work, in their places, as members of that body, they come to get something for themselves, as if there was nobody else's soul in the world to be saved but their own. Instead of coming to ask for the Spirit of God to deliver them from their selfishness, and make them care less about themselves, and more about all around them, they come to ask for the Spirit of

God because they think it will make themselves higher and happier in heaven. And of course they do not get what they come for, because they come for the wrong thing. Thus those who see them, begin to fancy that the Lord's Supper is not, after all, so very important for the salvation of their souls; and not finding in the Bible actually written these words, 'Thou shalt perish everlastingly unless thou take the Lord's Supper,' they end by staying away from it, and utterly neglecting it, they and their children after them; preferring their own selfishness, to God's Spirit of love, and saying, like Esau of old, 'I am hungry, and I must live. I must get on in this selfish world by following its selfish ways; what is the use of a spirit of love and brotherhood to me? If I were to obey the Gospel, and sacrifice my own interest for those around me, I should starve; what good will my birthright do me?

Oh! my friends, I pray God that some of you, at least, may change your mind. I pray God that some of you may see at last, that all the misery and the burdens of this time, spring from one root, which is selfishness; and that the reason why we are selfish, is because we have not with us the Spirit of God, which is the spirit of brotherhood and love. Let us pray God now, and henceforth, to take that selfishness out of all our hearts. Let us pray God now, and henceforth, to pour upon us, and upon all our countrymen, ay, and upon the whole world, the spirit of friendship and fellow-feeling, the spirit which when men have among them, they need no laws to keep them from supplanting, and oppressing, and devouring each other, because its fruits are love, cheerfulness, peace, long-suffering, gentleness, goodness, honesty, meekness, temperance. Then there will be no need, my friends, for me to call you to the Supper of the Lord. You will no more think of staying away from it, than the apostles did, when the Spirit was poured out on them. For what do we read that they did after the first Whit-Sunday? That altogether with one accord, they broke bread daily; that is, partook of the Lord's Supper every day, from house to house. They did not need to be told to do it. They did it, as I may say, by instinct. There was no question or argument about it in their minds. They had found out that they were all brothers, with one common cause in joy and sorrow—that they were all members of one body—that the life of their souls came from one root and spring, from one Lord and Saviour Jesus Christ, the light and the life of men, in whom they were all one, members of each other; and therefore, they delighted in that Lord's Supper, just because it brought them together; just because it was a sign and a token to them that they did belong to each other, that they had one Lord, one faith, one interest, one common cause for this life, and for all eternity. And therefore the blessing of that Lord's Supper did come to them, and in it they did receive strength to live like children of God, and members of Christ, and brothers to each other and to all mankind. They proved by their actions what that Communion Feast, that Sacrament of Brotherhood, had done for them. They proved it by not counting their own lives dear to them, but going forth in the face of poverty and persecution, and death itself, to preach to the whole world the good news that Christ was their King. They proved it by their conduct to each other when they had all things in common, and sold their possessions and goods, and parted them to all, as every man had need. They proved it by needing no laws to bind them to each other from without, because they were bound to each other from within, by the love which comes down from God, and is the very bond of peace, and of every virtue which becomes a man.

XI.

ASCENSION-DAY.

LUKE xxiv. 50—53.

And Jesus led them out as far as to Bethany; and he lifted up his hands and blessed them. And it came to pass while he blessed them, he was parted from them, and carried up into heaven. And they worshipped him and returned to Jerusalem, with great joy; and were continually in the temple, praising and blessing God.

ON this day it is fit and proper for us—if we have understood, and enjoyed, and profited by the wonder of the Lord's Ascension into heaven— to be in the same state of mind as the Apostles were after His Ascension: for what was right for them is right for us and for all men; the same effects which it produced on them it ought to produce on us. And we may know whether we are in the state in which Christian men ought to be, by seeing how far we are in the same state of mind as the Apostles were. Now the text tells us in what state of mind they were; how that, after the Lord Jesus was parted from them, and carried up into Heaven, they worshipped Him, and returned to Jerusalem, with great joy, and were continually in the temple, praising and blessing God. It seems at first sight certainly very strange that they should go back with great joy. They had just lost their Teacher, their Master—One who had been more to them than all friends and fathers could be; One who had taken them, poor simple fishermen, and changed the whole course of their lives, and taught them things which He had taught to no one else, and given them a great and awful work to do—the work of changing the ways and thoughts and doings of the whole world. He had sent them out —eleven unlettered working men—to fight against the sin and the misery of the whole world. And He had given them open warning of what they were to expect; that by it they should win neither credit, nor riches, nor ease, nor anything else that the world thinks worth having. He gave them fair warning that the world would hate them, and try to crush them. He told them, as the Gospel for to-day says, that they should be driven out of the churches; that the religious people, as well as the irreligious, would be against them; that the time would come when those who killed them would think that they did God service; that nothing but labour, and want, and persecution, and slander, and torture, and death was before them,—and now He had gone away and left them. He had vanished up into the empty air. They were to see His face, and hear His voice no more. They were to have no more of His advice, no more of His teaching, no more of His tender comfortings; they were to be alone in the world—eleven poor working men, with the whole world against them, and so great a business to do that they would not have time to get their bread by the labour of their hands. Is it not wonderful that they did not sit down in despair, and say, 'What will become of us?' Is it not wonderful that they did not give themselves up to grief at losing the Teacher who was worth all the rest of the world put together? Is it not wonderful that they did not go back, each one to his old trade, to his fishing and to his daily labour, saying, 'At all events we must eat; at all events we must get our livelihood;' and end, as they had begun, in being mere labouring men, of whom the world would never have heard a word? And instead of that we read that they went back with great joy not to their homes but to Jerusalem, the capital city of their country, and 'were continually in the temple blessing and praising God.' Well, my friends, and if it is possible for one man to judge what another man would have done—if it is possible to guess what we should have done in their case—common sense must show us this, that if He was merely their Teacher, they would have either given themselves up to despair, or gone back, some to their plough, some to their fishing-nets, and some, like Matthew, to their counting-houses, and we should never have heard a word of them. But if you will look in your Bibles, you will find that they thought Him much more than a teacher—that they thought Him to be the Lord and King of the whole world; and you will find that the great joy with which the disciples went back, after He ascended into heaven, came from certain very strange words that He had been speaking to them just before He ascended— words about which they could have but two opinions: —either they must have thought that they were utter falsehood, and self-conceit, and blasphemy; and that Jesus, who had been all along speaking to them such words of wisdom and holiness as never man spake before, had suddenly changed His whole character at the last, and become such a sort of person as it is neither fit for me to speak of, or you to hear me speak of, in God's church, and in Jesus Christ's hearing, even though it be merely for the sake of argument; or else they must have thought *this* about His words, that they were the most joyful and blessed words that ever had been spoken on the earth; that they were the best of all news; the most complete of all Gospels for this poor sinful world; that what Jesus had said about Himself was true; and that as long as it was true, it did not matter in the least what became of them; it did not matter in the least what difficulties stood in their way, for they would be certain to conquer them all; it did not matter in the least how men might persecute and slander them, for they would be sure to get their reward; it did not matter in the least how miserable and sinful the world might be just then, for it was certain to be changed, and converted, and brought to God, to righteousness, to love, to freedom, to light, at last.

If you look at the various accounts, in the four gospels, of the Lord's last words on earth, you will see, surely, what I mean. Let us take them one by one.

St. Matthew tells us that, a few days before the Lord's ascension, He met His disciples on a mountain in Galilee, where He had appointed them to await Him; and there told them, that all power was given to Him in heaven and earth. Was not that blessed news—was not that a gospel? That all the power in heaven and earth belonged to *Him?* To Him, who had all His life been doing good? To Him, in whom there had never been one single stain of tyranny or selfishness? To Him, who had been the friend of publicans and sinners? To Him, who had rebuked the very richest, and loved the very poorest? To Him, who had shown that He had both the power and the will to

ASCENSION-DAY. 135

heal every kind of sickness and disease ? To Him, who had conquered and driven out, wherever He met them, all the evil spirits which enslave and torment poor sinful men ? To Him, who had shown by rising from the dead, that He was stronger than even death itself? To Him, who had declared that He was the Son of God the Father, that the great God who had made heaven and earth, and all therein, was perfectly pleased and satisfied with Him, that He was come to do His Father's will, and not His own; that He was the ancient Lord of the earth, the I AM who was before Abraham ? And He was now to have all power in heaven and earth ! Everything which was done right in the world henceforth, was to be his doing. The kingdom and rule over the whole universe, was to be His. So He said ; and His disciples believed Him; and if they believed Him, how could they but rejoice ? How could they but rejoice at the glorious thought that He, the son of the village maiden, the champion of the poor and the suffering, was to have the government of the world for ever? That He, who all the while He had been on earth had showed that He was perfect justice, perfect love, perfect humanity, was to reign till He had put all His enemies under His feet ? How could the world but prosper under such a King as that ? How could wickedness triumph, while He, the perfectly righteous one, was King? How could misery triumph, while He, the perfectly merciful one, was King? How could ignorance triumph, while He, the perfectly wise one, who had declared that God the Father hid nothing from Him, was King? Unless the disciples had been more dull and selfish than the dumb beasts around them, what could they do but rejoice at that news? What matter to them if Jesus were taken out of their sight, as long as all power was given to Him in heaven and earth?

But He had told them more. He had told them that they were not to keep this glorious secret to themselves. No: they were to go forth and preach the gospel of it, the good news of it, to every creature—to preach the gospel of the kingdom of God. The good news that God was the King of men, after all; that cruel tyrants and oppressors, and conquerors, were not their kings; that neither the storms over their heads, nor the earth under their feet, nor the clouds and the rivers whom the heathens used to worship in the hope of persuading the earth and the weather to be favourable to them, and bless their harvests, were their kings; that idols of wood and stone, and evil spirits of lust, and cruelty, and covetousness, were not their kings; but that God was their King;

ASCENSION-DAY.

that He loved them, He pitied them in spite of all their sins; that He had sent His only begotten Son into the world to teach them, to live for them, —to die for them—to claim them for His own. And, therefore, they were to go and baptize all nations, as a sign that they were to repent, and change, and put away all their old, false, and evil heathen life, and rise to a new life, they and their children after them, as God's children, God's family, brothers of the Son of God. And they were to baptize them into a name; showing that they belonged to those into whose name they were baptized; into the name of the Father, and the Son, and the Holy Spirit. They were to be baptized into the name of the Father, as a sign that God was their Father, and they His children. They were to be baptized into the name of the Son, as a sign that the Son, Jesus Christ, was their King and head; and not merely their King and head, but their Saviour, who had taken away the sin of the world, and redeemed it for God, with His own most precious blood; and not merely their Saviour, but their pattern; that they might know that they were bound to become as far as is possible for mortal man, such sons of God as Jesus himself had been, like Him obedient, pure, forgiving, brotherly, caring for each other and not for themselves, doing their heavenly Father's will and not their own.

And they were to baptize all nations into the name of the Holy Spirit, for a sign that God's Spirit, the Lord and giver of life, would be with them, to give them new life, new holiness, new manfulness; to teach, and guide, and strengthen them for ever. That was the gospel which they had to preach. The good news that the Son of God was the King of men. That was the name into which they were to baptize all nations—the name of children of God, members of Christ, heirs of a heavenly and spiritual kingdom, which should go on age after age, for ever, growing and spreading men knew not how, as the grains of mustard-seed, which at first the least of all seeds, grows up into a great tree, and the birds of the air come and lodge in the branches of it—to go on, I say, from age to age, improving, cleansing, and humanizing, and teaching the whole world, till the kingdoms of the earth became the kingdoms of God and of His Christ. That was the work which the apostles had given them to do. Do you not see, friends, that unless those apostles had been the most selfish of men, unless all they cared for was their own gain and comfort, they must have rejoiced? The whole world was to be set right—what matter what happened to them? And, therefore, I said at the beginning of my sermon, that a sure way to know whether our minds were in a right state, was to see whether we felt about it as the apostles felt. The Bible tells us to rejoice always, to praise and give thanks to God always. If we believe what the apostles believed, we shall be joyful; if we do not, we shall not be joyful. If we believe in the words which the Lord spoke before He ascended on high, we shall be joyful. If we believe that all power in heaven and earth is His, we shall be joyful. If we believe that the son of the village maiden has ascended up on high, and received gifts for men, we shall be joyful. If we believe that, as our baptism told us, God is our Father, the Son of God our Saviour, the Spirit of God ready to teach and guide us, we shall be joyful. Do you answer me, 'But the world goes on so ill: there is so much sin and misery, and folly, and cruelty in it: how can we be joyful?' I answer—There was a hundred times as much sin, and misery, and folly, and cruelty in the world, in the apostles' time, and yet they were joyful, and full of gladness, blessing and praising God. If you answer, 'But we are so slandered, and neglected, and misunderstood, and hard-worked, and ill-treated; we have no time to enjoy ourselves, or do the things which we should like best. How can we be joyful?' I answer—So were the apostles. They knew that they would be a hundred times as much slandered, and neglected, and misunderstood, as you can ever be ; that they would have far less time to enjoy themselves, far less opportunity of doing the things which they liked best, than you can ever have : they knew that misery, and persecution, and a shameful death were before them, and yet they were joyful and full of gladness, blessing and praising God. And why should you not be ? For what was true for them is true for you. They had no blessing, no hope, but what you have just as good a right to as they had. They were joyful, because God was their father ; and God is your father. They were joyful, because they and all men belonged to God's family ; and you belong to it. They were joyful, because God's Spirit was promised to them, to make them like God ; and God's Spirit was promised to you. They were joyful, because a poor man was king of heaven and earth ; and that poor man, Jesus Christ, who was born at Bethlehem, is as much your King now as He was theirs then. They were joyful, because the whole world was going to improve under His rule and government ; and the whole world is improving, and will go on improving for ever. They were joyful because Jesus, whom they had known as a poor, despised, crucified man on earth, had ascended up to heaven in glory ; and if you believe the same, you will be joyful too. In proportion as you believe the mystery of

Ascension-day; if you believe the words which the Lord spoke before He ascended, you will have cheerful, joyful, hopeful thoughts about yourselves, and about the whole world; if you do not, you will be in continual danger of becoming suspicious and despairing, fancying the world still worse than it is, fancying that God has neglected and forgotten it, fancying that the devil is stronger than God, and man's sins wider than Christ's redemption, till you will think it neither worth while to do right yourselves, nor to make others do right towards you.

XII.

THE FOUNT OF SCIENCE.

A SERMON

PREACHED AT ST. MARGARET'S CHURCH, WESTMINSTER,
MAY 4, 1851,
IN BEHALF OF THE WESTMINSTER HOSPITAL.

PSALM lxviii. 18, and EPHESIANS iv. 8.

When He ascended up on high, He led captivity captive, and received gifts for men, yea, even for his enemies, that the Lord God might dwell among them.

IF, a thousand years ago, a congregation in this place had been addressed upon the text which I have chosen, they would have had, I think, little difficulty in applying its meaning to themselves, and in mentioning at once innumerable instances of those gifts which the King of men had received for men, innumerable signs that the Lord God was really dwelling amongst them. But amongst those signs, I think, they would have mentioned several which we are not now generally accustomed to consider in such a light. They would have pointed not merely to the building of churches, the founding of schools, the spread of peace, the decay of slavery; but to the importation of foreign literature, the extension of the arts of reading, writing, painting, architecture, the improvement of agriculture, and the introduction of new and more successful methods of the cure of diseases. They might have expressed themselves on these points in a way that we consider now puerile and superstitious. They might have attributed to the efficacy of prayer, many cures which we now attribute —shall I say? to no cause whatsoever. They may have quoted as an instance of St. Cuthbert's sanctity, rather than of his shrewd observations, his discovery of a spring of water in the rocky floor of his cell, and his success in growing barley upon the barren island where wheat refused to germinate; and we might have smiled at their superstition, and smiled, too, at their seeing any consequence of Christianity, any token that the kingdom of God was among them, in Bishop Wilfred's rescuing the Hampshire Saxons from the horrors of famine, by teaching them the use of fishing-nets. But still so they would have spoken—men of a turn of mind no less keen, shrewd, and practical than we, their children; and if we had objected to their so-called superstition that all these improvements in the physical state of England were only the natural consequences of the introduction of Roman civilization by French and Italian missionaries, they would have smiled at us in their turn, not perhaps without some astonishment at our stupidity, and asked, 'Do you not see, too, that *that* is in itself a sign of the kingdom of God—that these nations who have been for ages selfishly isolated from each other, except for purposes of conquest and desolation, should be now teaching each other, helping each other, interchanging more and more, generation by generation, their arts, their laws, their learning becoming fused down under the influence of a common Creed, and loyalty to one common King in heaven, from their state of savage jealousy and warfare, into one great Christendom, and family of God? And if, my friends, as I think, those forefathers of ours could rise from their graves this day, they would be inclined to see in our hospitals, in our railroads, in the achievements of our physical science, confirmation of that old superstition of theirs, proofs of the kingdom of God, realizations of the gifts which Christ received for men, vaster than any of which they had ever dreamed. They might be startled at God's continuing those gifts to us,.who hold on many points a creed so different from theirs. They might be still more startled to see in the Great Exhibition of all Nations, which is our present nine-days' wonder, that those blessings were not restricted by God even to nominal Christians, but that His love,

His teaching, with regard to matters of civilization and physical science, were extended, though more slowly and partially, to the Mahometan and the Heathen. And it would be a wholesome lesson to them, to find that God's grace was wider than their narrow theories; perhaps they may have learnt it already in the world of spirits. But of its *being* God's grace, there would be no doubt in their minds. They would claim unhesitatingly, and at once, that great Exhibition established in a Christian country, as a point of union and brotherhood for all people, for a sign that God was indeed claiming all the nations of the world as His own— proving by the most enormous facts that He had sent down a Pentecost, gifts to men which would raise them not merely spiritually, but physically and intellectually, beyond anything which the world had ever seen, and had poured out a spirit among them which would convert them in the course of ages, gradually, but most surely and really, from a pandemonium of conquerors and conquered, devourers and devoured, into a family of fellow-helping brothers, until the kingdoms of the world became the kingdoms of God and of His Christ.

But I think, one thing, if anything, would stagger their simple old Saxon faith; one thing would make them fearful, as indeed it makes the preacher this day, that the time of real brotherhood and peace is still but too far off; and that the achievements of our physical science, the unity of this great Exhibition, noble as they are, are still only dim forecastings, and prophecies as it were, of a higher, nobler reality. And they would say sadly to us, their children, 'Sons, you ought to be so near to God: He seems to have given you so much, and to have worked among you as he never worked for any nation under heaven :—How is it that you give the glory to yourselves, and not to Him ?'

For do we give the glory of our scientific discoveries to God, in any real, honest, and practical sense ? There may be some official and perfunctory talk of God's blessing on our endeavours: but there seems to be no real belief in us that God, the inspiration of God, is the very fount and root of the endeavours themselves; that He teaches us these great discoveries ; that He gives us wisdom to get this wondrous wealth ; that He works in us to will and to do of his good pleasure. True, we keep up something of the form and tradition of the old talk about such things; we join in prayer to God to bless our Great Exhibition ; but we do not believe —we do not believe, my friends—that it was God who taught us to conceive, build, and arrange that Great Exhibition ; and our notion of God's blessing it, seems to be God's absence from it; a hope and trust that God will leave it and us alone, and not 'visit' it or us in it, or 'interfere' by any 'special providences,' by storms, or lightning, or sickness, or panic, or conspiracy; a sort of dim feeling that we could manage it all perfectly well without God, but that as He exists, and has some power over natural phenomena, which is not very exactly defined, we must notice His existence over and above our work, lest He should become angry, and 'visit' us. . . . And this in spite of words which were spoken by one whose office it was to speak them, as the representative of the highest and most sacred personage in these realms; words which deserve to be written in letters of gold on the high places of this city; in which he spoke of this Exhibition as an 'approach to a more complete fulfilment of the great and sacred mission which man has to perform in the world;' when he told the English people, that 'man's reason being created in the image of God, he has to discover the laws by which Almighty God governs His creations, and by making these laws the standard of his action, to conquer nature to his use, himself a divine instrument;' when he spoke of 'thankfulness to Almighty God for what he has already *given*,' as the first feeling which that Exhibition ought to excite in us; and as the second, 'the deep conviction that those blessings can only be realized in proportion to'—not, as some would have it, the rivalry and selfish competition—but 'in proportion to the *help* which we are prepared to render to each other ; and, therefore, by peace, love, and ready assistance, not only between individuals, but between all nations of the earth.' We read those great words; but in the hearts of how few, alas! to judge from our modern creed on such matters, must the really important and distinctive points of them find an echo! To how few does this whole Exhibition seem to have been anything but a matter of personal gain or curiosity, for national aggrandizement, insular self-glorification, and selfish—I had almost said, treacherous—rivalry with the very foreigners whom we invited as our guests?

And so, too, with our cures of diseases. We speak of God's blessing the means, and God's blessing the cure. But all we really mean by blessing them, is permitting them. Do not our hearts confess that our notion of His blessing the means, is His leaving the means to themselves, and their own physical laws—leaving, in short, the cure to us and not preventing our science doing its work, and asserting his own existence by bringing on some unexpected crisis, or unfortunate relapse—if indeed the old theory that He does bring on such, be true?

Our old forefathers, on the other hand, used to

THE FOUNT OF SCIENCE. 149

believe that in medicine, as in everything else, God taught men all that they knew. They believed the words of The Wise Man when he said that 'The Spirit of God gives man understanding.' The method by which Solomon believed himself to have obtained all his physical science and knowledge of trees, from the cedar of Lebanon to the hyssop which groweth on the wall, was in their eyes the only possible method. They believed the words of Isaiah when he said of the tillage, and the rotation of crops in use among the peasants of his country, that their God instructed them to discretion and taught them ; and that even the various methods of threshing out the various species of grain, came 'forth from the Lord of hosts, who is excellent in counsel, and wonderful in working.' . . . .

Such a method, you say, seems to you now miraculous. It did not seem to our forefathers miraculous that God should teach man ; it seemed to them most simple, most rational, most natural, an utterly every-day axiom. They thought it was because so few of the heathen were taught by God that they were no wiser than they were. They thought that since the Son of God had come down and taken our nature upon Him, and ascended up on high and received gifts for men, that it was now the right and privilege of every human being who was willing, to be taught of God, as the prophet foretold in those very words; and that baptism was the very sign and seal of that fact—a sign that for every human being, whatever his age, sex, rank, intellect, or race, a certain measure of the teaching of God and of the Spirit of God was ready, promised, sure as the oath of Him that made heaven and the earth, and all things therein. That was Solomon's belief. We do not find that it made him a fanatic and an idler, waiting with folded hands for inspiration to come to him he knew not how nor whence. His belief that wisdom was the revelation and gift of God did not prevent him from seeking her as silver, and searching for her as hid treasures, from applying his heart to seek and search out by wisdom concerning all things that are done under heaven; and we do not find that it prevented our forefathers. Ceadmon's belief that God inspired him with the poetic faculty, did not make him the less laborious and careful versifier. Bishop John's blessing the dumb boy's tongue in the name of Him whom he believed to be Word of God and the Master of that poor dumb boy, did not prevent his anticipating some of the discoveries of our modern wise men, in setting about a most practical and scientific cure. Alfred's continual prayers for light and inspiration made him no less a laborious and thoughtful student of war and law, of physics, language, and geography. Those old Teutons, for all these superstitions of theirs, were perhaps as businesslike and practical in those days as we their children are in these. But that did not prevent their believing that unless God showed them a thing, they could not see it, and thanking Him honestly enough for the comparative little which He did show them. But we who enjoy the accumulated teaching of ages—we to whose researches He is revealing year by year, almost week by week, wonders of which they never dreamed—we whom He has taught to make the lame to walk, the dumb to speak, the blind to see, to exterminate the pestilence and defy the thunderbolt, to multiply millionfold the fruits of learning, to annihilate time and space, to span the heavens, and to weigh the sun—what madness is this which has come upon us in these last days, to make us fancy that we, insects of a day, have found out these things for ourselves, and talk big about the progress of the species, and the triumphs of intellect, and the all-conquering powers of the human mind, and give the glory of all this inspiration and revelation, not to God, but to ourselves? Let us beware, beware—lest our boundless pride and self-satisfaction, by some mysterious yet most certain law, avenge itself—lest like the Assyrian conqueror of old, while we stand and cry, 'Is not this great

Babylon which I have built?' our reason, like his, should reel and fall beneath the narcotic of our own maddening self-conceit, and while attempting to scale the heavens we overlook some pitfall at our feet, and fall as learned idiots, suicidal pedants, to be a degradation, and a hissing, and a shame.

However strongly you may differ from these opinions of our own forefathers with regard to the ground and cause of physical science, and the arts of healing, I am sure that the recollection of the thrice holy ground upon which we stand, beneath the shadow of venerable piles, witnesses for the creeds, the laws, the liberties, which those our ancestors have handed down to us, will preserve you from the temptation of dismissing with hasty contempt their thoughts upon any subject so important; will make you inclined to listen to their opinion with affection, if not with reverence; and save, perhaps, the preacher from a sneer when he declares that the doctrine of those old Saxon men is, in his belief, not only the most Scriptural, but the most rational and scientific explanation of the grounds of all human knowledge.

At least I shall be able to quote in support of my own opinion a name from which there can be no appeal in the minds of a congregation of educated Englishmen—I mean Francis Bacon, Lord

THE FOUNT OF SCIENCE. 153

Verulam, the spiritual father of the modern science, and, therefore, of the chemistry and the medicine of the whole civilized world. If there is one thing which more than another ought to impress itself on the mind of a careful student of his works, it is this—that he considered science as the inspiration of God, and every separate act of induction by which man arrives at a physical law, as a revelation from the Maker of those laws; and that the faith which gave him daring to face the mystery of the universe, and proclaim to men that they could conquer nature by obeying her, was his deep, living, practical belief that there was One who had ascended up on high, and led captive in the flesh and spirit of a man those very idols of sense which had been themselves leading men's minds captive, enslaving them to the illusions of their own senses, forcing them to bow down in vague awe and terror before those powers of Nature, which God had appointed, not to be their tyrants, but their slaves. I will not special-plead particulars from his works, wherein I may consider that he asserts this. I will rather say boldly that the idea runs through every line he ever wrote; that unless seen in the light of that faith, the grounds of his philosophy ought to be as inexplicable to us, as they would, without it, have been impossible to himself. As has been well said of him, 'Faith in God as the absolute ground of all human as well as of all natural laws; the belief that He had actually made Himself known to His creatures, and that it was possible for them to have a knowledge of Him, cleared from the phantasies and idols of their own imaginations and understandings; this was the necessary foundation of all that great man's mind and speculations, to whatever point they were tending, and however at times they might be darkened by too close a familiarity with the corruptions and meannesses of man, or too passionate an addiction to the contemplation of Nature. Nor should it ever be forgotten that he owed all the clearness and distinctness of his mind to his freedom from that Pantheism which naturally disposes to a vague admiration and adoration of Nature, to the belief that it is stronger and nobler than ourselves; that we are servants, and puppets, and portions of it, and not its lords and rulers. If Bacon had in anywise confounded Nature with God—if he had not entertained the strongest practical feeling that men were connected with God through One who had taken upon Him their nature, it is impossible that he could have discovered that method of dealing with physics, which has made a physical science possible.'

No really careful student of his works, but must

have perceived this, however glad, alas! he may have felt at times to thrust the thought of it from him, and try to think that Francis Bacon's Christianity was something over and above his philosophy—a religion which he left behind him at the church-door—or only sprinkled up and down his works so much of it as should shield him in a bigoted age from the suspicion of materialism.— A strange theory, and yet one which, so determined is man to see nothing, whether it be in the Bible or in the Novum Organum, but what each wishes to see, has been deliberately put forth again and again by men who fancy, forsooth, that the greatest of English heroes was even such an one as themselves. One does not wonder to find among the general characteristics of those writers who admire Bacon as a materialist, the most utter incapacity of philosophising on Bacon's method, the very restless conceit, the hasty generalization, the hankering after cosmogonic theories, which Bacon anathematizes in every page—Yes, I repeat it, we owe our medical and sanitary science to Bacon's philosophy; and Bacon owed his philosophy to his Christianity.

Oh! it is easy for us, amid the marvels of our great hospitals, now grown commonplace in our eyes from very custom, to talk of the empire of mind over matter; for us—who reap the harvest whereof Bacon sowed the seed. But consider, how great the faith of that man must have been, who died in hope, not having received the promises, but seeing them afar off, and haunted to his dying day with glorious visions of a time when famine and pestilence should vanish before a scientific obedience—to use his own expression—to the will of God, revealed in natural facts. Thus we can understand how he dared to denounce all that had gone before him as blind and worthless guides, and to proclaim himself to the world as the one restorer of true physical philosophy. Thus we can understand how he, the cautious and patient man of the world, dared indulge in those vast dreams of the scientific triumphs of the future. Thus we can understand how he dared hint at the expectation that men would some day even conquer death itself; because he believed that man had conquered death already, in the person of its King and Lord—in the flesh of Him who ascended up on high, and led captivity captive, and received gifts for men. The 'empire of mind over matter?' What practical proof had he of it amid the miserable alternations of empiricism and magic which made up the pseudo-science of his time; amid the theories and speculations of mankind, which as he said, were 'but a sort of madness—useless alike for discovery or for operation.' What right had he, more than any other man who had gone before him, to believe that man could conquer and mould to his will the unseen and tremendous powers which work in every cloud and every flower? that he could dive into the secret mysteries of his own body, and renew his youth like the eagle's? This ground he had for that faith—that he believed, as he says himself, that he must 'begin from God; and that the pursuit of physical science clearly proceeds from Him, the Author of good, and Father of light.' This gave him faith to say that in this, as in all other Divine works, the smallest beginnings lead assuredly to some result, and that the 'remark in spiritual matters, that the kingdom of God cometh without observation, is also found to be true in every great work of Divine Providence; so that everything glides on quietly without confusion or noise, and the matter is achieved before men either think or perceive that it is commenced.' This it was which gave him courage to believe that his own philosophy might be the actual fulfilment of the prophecy, that in the last days many should run to and fro, and knowledge should be increased—words which, like hundreds of others in his works, sound like the outpourings of an almost blasphemous self-conceit, till we recollect that he looked on science only as the inspiration of God, and man's empire over nature only as the consequence of the redemption worked out for him by Christ, and begin to see in them the expressions of the deepest and most divine humility.

I doubt not that many here will be far more able than I am practically to apply the facts which I have been adducing to the cause of the hospital for which I am pleading. But there is one consequence of them to which I must beg leave to draw your attention more particularly, especially at the present era of our nation. If, then, these discoveries of science be indeed revelations and inspirations from God, does it not follow that all classes, even the poorest and the most ignorant, the most brutal, have an equal right to enjoy the fruits of them? Does it not follow that to give to the poor their share in the blessings which chemical and medical science are working out for us, is not a matter of charity or benevolence, but of *duty*, of indefeasible, peremptory, immediate duty? For consider, my friends; the Son of God descends on earth, and takes on Him not only the form, but the very nature, affections, trials, and sorrows of a man. He proclaims Himself as the person who has been all along ruling, guiding, teaching, improving men; the light who lighteth every man who cometh into the world. He proclaims Himself by acts of wondrous power to be the internecine foe and conqueror of every form of sorrow, slavery, barbarism, weakness, sickness, death itself. He proclaims Himself as One who is come to give His life for His sheep—One who is come to restore to men the likeness in which they were originally created, the likeness of their Father in Heaven, who accepteth the person of no man—who causeth His sun to shine on the evil and on the good, who sendeth his rain on the just and on the unjust, in whose sight the meanest publican, if his only consciousness be that of his own baseness and worthlessness, is more righteous than the most learned, respectable, and self-satisfied pharisee. He proclaims Himself the setter-up of a Kingdom into which the publican and the harlot will pass sooner than the rich, the mighty, and the noble; a kingdom in which all men are to be brothers, and their bond of union, loyalty to One who spared not His own life for the sheep, who came not to do His own, but the will of the Father who had sent Him, and who showed by His toil among the poor, the outcast, the ignorant, and the brutal, what that same will was like. With His own life-blood He seals this Covenant between God and man. He offers up His own body as the first-fruits of this great kingdom of self-sacrifice. He takes poor fishermen and mechanics, and sends them forth to acquaint all men with the good news that God is their King, and to baptize them as subjects of that kingdom, bound to rise in baptism to a new life, a life of love, and brotherhood, and self-sacrifice, like His own. He commands them to call all nations to that sacred Feast wherein there is neither rich nor poor, but the same bread and the same wine are offered to the monarch and to the slave, as signs of their common humanity, their common redemption, their common interest—signs that they derive their life, their health, their reason, their every faculty of body, soul, and spirit, from One who walked the earth as the son of a poor carpenter, who ate and drank with publicans and sinners. He sends down His Spirit on them with gifts of language, eloquence, wisdom, and healing, as mere earnests and first-fruits; so they said, of that prophecy that He would pour out His Spirit upon all flesh, even upon slaves and handmaids. And these poor fishermen feel themselves impelled by a divine and irresistible impulse to go forth to the ends of the world, and face persecution, insult, torture and death—not in order that they may make themselves lords over mankind, but that they may tell them that One is their Master, even Jesus Christ, both God and man—that *He* rules the world, and will rule it, and *can* rule it, that in His sight there is no distinction of race, or rank, or riches, neither Jew nor Greek, barbarian, Scythian, bond or free.. And, as a fact, their message has prevailed and been believed; and in proportion as it has prevailed, not merely individual sanctity or piety, but liberty, law, peace, civilization, learning, art, science, the gifts which He bought for men with His blood, have followed in its train :—while the nations who have not received that message that God was their King, or having received it have forgotten it, or perverted it into a superstition and an hypocrisy, have in exactly that proportion fallen back into barbarism and bloodshed, slavery and misery. My friends, if this philosophy of history, this theory of human progress, or as I should call it, this Gospel of the Kingdom of God mean anything—does it not mean this? this which our forefathers believed, dimly and inconsistently perhaps, but still believed it, else we had not been here this day—that we are not our own, but the servants of Jesus Christ, and brothers of each other—that the very constitution and ground-law of this human species which has been redeemed by Christ, is the self-sacrifice which Christ displayed as the one perfection of humanity—that all rank, property, learning, science, are only held by their possessors in trust from that King who has distributed them to each according as He will, that each might use them for the good of all, certain— as certain as God's promise can make man—that if by giving up our own interest for the interest of others, we seek first the kingdom of God, and the righteousness between man and man, which we call *mercy*, according to which it is constituted, all other things, health, wealth, peace, and every other blessing which humanity can desire, shall be added unto us over and above, as the natural and necessary fruits of a society founded according to the will of God, and declared in his Son Jesus Christ, and therefore according to those physical laws, whereof he is at once the Creator, the Director, and the Revealer?

This was the faith of our forefathers, both laity and clergy—that the Lord was King, be the people never so unquiet; that men were His stewards and His pupils only, and not his vicars; that they were equal in His sight, and not the slaves and tyrants of each other; and that the help that was done upon earth, He did it all Himself. Dimly, doubtless, they saw it, and inconsistently: but they saw it, and to their faith in that great truth we owe all that has made England really noble among the nations. Of the fruits of that faith every venerable building around us should remind us. To that faith in the laity, we owe the abolition of serfdom, the freedom of our institutions, the laws which provide equal justice between man and man; to that faith in the clergy, and especially in the monastic orders, we owe the endowment of our schools and universities, the improvement of agriculture, the preservation and the spread of all the liberal arts and sciences, as far as they were then discovered; so that every one of those abbeys which we now revile so ignorantly, became a centre of freedom, protection, healing and civilization, a refuge for the oppressed, a well-spring of mercy for the afflicted, a practical witness to the nation that property and science were not the private and absolute possession of men, but only held in trust from God for the benefit of the common weal: and just in proportion as in the 14th and 15th centuries those institutions fell from their first estate, and began to fancy that their wealth and wisdom was their own, acquired by their own cunning, to be used for their own aggrandizement, they became an imposture and an imbecility, an abomination and a ruin. And it was this faith, too, in a still nobler and clearer form, which at the Reformation inspired the age which could produce a Ridley, a Latimer, an Elizabeth, a Shakspeare, a Spencer, a Raleigh, a Bacon, and a Milton; which knit together, in spite of religious feuds and social wrongs, the nation of England with a bond which all the powers of hell endeavoured in vain to break. Doubtless, there too there was inconsistency enough. Elizabeth may have mixed up ambitious dynastic dreams with her intense belief that God had given her her wisdom, her learning, her mighty will, only to be the servant of His servants and defender of the faith. Men like Drake and Raleigh, while they were believing that God had sent them forth to smite with the sword of the Lord the devourers of the earth, the destroyers of religion, freedom, civilization and national life, may have been unfaithful to what they believed their divine mission, and fancied that they might use the wisdom and valour that God gave them for their selfish ends, till they committed (as some say) acts of rapacity and cruelty worthy of the merest buccaneer. But *that* was not what made them conquer—that was not what made the wealth and the might of Spain melt away before their little bands of heroes; but the same old faith, shining out in all their noblest acts and words, that 'the Lord *was* King, and that the help that was done upon earth, He did it all Himself.' So again, Bacon may have fancied, and did fancy in his old age, that he might use his deep knowledge of mankind for his own selfish ends—that he might indulge himself in building himself up a name that might fill all the earth, that he who had done so much for God and for mankind, might be allowed to do at last somewhat for himself, and tempted, by a paltry bribe, fall for awhile, as David did before him, that God, and not he, might have the glory of all his wisdom. But then he was less than himself; then he had but lost sight of his lode-star. Then he had forgotten, but only for a while, that he owed all to the teaching of that God who had given to the young and obscure advocate the mission of affecting the destinies of nations yet unborn.

And believe me, my friends, even as it has been with our forefathers, so it will be with us. According to our faith will it be unto us, now as it was of old. In proportion as we believe that wealth, science, and civilization are the work and property of man, in just that proportion we shall be tempted to keep them selfishly and exclusively to ourselves. The man of science will be tempted to hide his discoveries, though men may be perishing for lack of them, till he can sell them to the highest bidder; the rich man will be tempted to purchase them for himself, in order that he may increase his own comfort and luxury, and feel comparatively lazy and careless about their application to the welfare of the masses; he will be tempted to pay an exorbitant price for anything that can increase his personal convenience, and yet when the question is about improving the supply of necessaries to the poor, stand haggling about considerations of profitable investment, excuse himself from doing the duty which lies nearest to him by visions of distant profit, of which a thousand unexpected accidents may deprive him after all, and make his boasted scientific care for the wealth of the nation an excuse for leaving tens of thousands worse housed and worse fed than his own beasts of burden. The poor man will be tempted frantically to oppose his selfishness and unbelief to the selfishness and unbelief of the rich, and clutch from him by force the comforts which really belong to neither of them, in order that he may pride himself in them and misuse them in his turn ; and the clergy will be tempted, as they have too often been tempted already, to fancy that reason is the enemy, and not the twin sister of faith ; to oppose revelation to science, as if God's two messages could contradict each other ; to widen the Manichæan distinction between secular and spiritual matters, so pleasant to the natural atheism of fallen man ; to fancy that they honour God by limiting as much as possible His teaching, His providence, His wisdom, His love, and His kingdom, and to pretend that they are defending the creeds of the Catholic Church, by denying to them any practical or real influence on the economic, political, and physical welfare of mankind. But in proportion as we hold to the old faith of our forefathers concerning science and civilization, we shall feel it not only a duty, but a glory and a delight, to make all men sharers in them ; to go out into the streets and lanes of the city and call in the maimed, and the halt, and the blind, that they may sit down and take their share of the good things which God has provided in His kingdom for those who obey Him. Every new discovery will be hailed by us as a fresh boon from God to be bestowed by the rain and the sunshine freely upon us all. The sight of every sufferer will make us ready to suspect and to examine ourselves lest we should be in some indirect way the victim of some neglect or selfishness of our own. Every disease will be a sign to us that in some respect or other, the physical or moral laws of human nature have been overlooked or broken. The existence of an unhealthy locality, the recurrence of an epidemic, will be to us a subject of public shame and self-reproach. Men of science will no longer go up and down entreating mankind in vain to make use of their discoveries; the sanitary reformer will be no longer like Wisdom crying in the streets and no man regarding her; and in every ill to which flesh is heir we shall see an enemy of our King and Lord, and an intruder into His kingdom, against which we swore at our baptism to fight with an inspiring and delicious certainty that God will prosper the right; that His laws cannot change; that nature, and the disturbances and poisons, and brute powers thereof, were meant to be the slaves and not the tyrants of a race whose head has conquered the grave itself.

This is no speculative dream. The progress of science is daily proving it to be an actual truth; proving to us that a large proportion of diseases—how large a proportion, no man yet dare say—are preventible by science under the direction of that common justice and mercy which man owes to man. The proper cultivation of the soil, it is now clearly seen, will exterminate fevers and agues, and all the frightful consequences of malaria. An attention to those simple decencies and cleanlinesses of life of which even the wild animals feel the necessity, will prevent the epidemics of our cities, and all the frightful train of secondary diseases which follow them, or supply their place. The question which is generally more and more forcing itself on the minds of scientific men is not how many diseases are, but how few are not, the consequences of man's ignorance, barbarism, and folly. The medical man is felt more and more to be as necessary in health as he is in sickness, to be the fellow-workman not merely of the clergyman, but of the social reformer, the political economist, and the statesman ; and the first object of his science to be prevention, and not cure. But if all this be true, as true it is, we ought to begin to look on Hospitals as many medical men I doubt not do already, in a sadder though in a no less important light. When we remember that the majority of cases which fill their wards are cases of more or less directly preventible diseases, the fruits of our social neglect, too often of our neglect of the sufferers themselves, too often also our neglect of their parents and forefathers; when we think how many a bitter pang is engendered and propagated from generation to generation in the noisome alleys and courts of this metropolis, by foul food, foul bed-rooms, foul air, foul water, by intemperance, the natural and almost pardonable consequence of want of water, depressing and degrading employ-ments, and lives spent in such an atmosphere of filth as our daintier nostrils could not endure a day: then we should learn to look upon these Hospitals not as acts of charity, supererogatory benevolences of ours towards those to whom we owe nothing, but as confessions of sin, and worthy fruits of penitence; as poor and late and partial compensation for misery which we might have prevented. And when again, taking up scientific works, we find how vast a pro-portion of the remaining cases of disease are pro-duced directly or indirectly by the unhealthiness of certain occupations, so certainly that the scientific man can almost prophesy the average shortening of life, and the peculiar form of disease, incident to any given form of city labour—when we find, to quote a single instance, that a large proportion— one half, as I am informed—of the female cases in certain Hospitals, are those of women-servants suffering from diseases produced by overwork in household labour, especially by carrying heavy weights up the steep stairs of our London houses—when we consider the large proportion of accident cases which are the result, if not always of neglect in our social arrangements, still of danger incurred in labouring for us, we shall begin to feel that our debt towards the poorer classes, for whom this and other Hospitals are instituted, swells and mounts up to a burden wh ich ught to be and would be intolerable to us, if we had not some such means as this Hospital affords of testifying our contrition for neglect for which we cannot atone, and of practically claiming in the Hospital our brotherhood with those masses whom we pass by so carelessly in the workshop and the street. What matters it that they have undertaken a life of labour from necessity, and with a full consciousness of the dangers they incur in it? For whom have they been labouring, but for us? Their handywork renders our houses luxurious. We wear the clothes they make. We eat the food they produce. They sit in darkness and the shadow of death that we may enjoy light and life and luxury and civilization. True, they are free men, in name, not free though from the iron necessity of crushing toil. Shall we make their liberty a cloak for our licentiousness? and because they are our brothers and

THE FOUNT OF SCIENCE. 171

not our slaves, answer with Cain, 'Am I my brother's keeper?' What if we have paid them the wages which they ask? We do not feed our beasts of burden only as long as they are in health, and when they fall sick leave them to cure themselves and starve—and these are not our beasts of burden; they are members of Christ, children of God, inheritors of the Kingdom of Heaven. Prove it to them, then, for they are in bitter danger of forgetting it in these days. Prove to them, by helping to cure their maladies, that they are members of Christ, that they do indeed belong to Him who without fee or payment freely cured the sick of Judea in old time. Prove to them that they are children of God, by treating them as such—as children of Him without whom not a sparrow falls to the ground, children of Him whose love is over all His works, children of Him who defends the widow and the fatherless, and sees that those who are in need or necessity have right, and who maketh inquiry for the blood of the innocent. Prove to them that they are inheritors of the Kingdom of Heaven, by proving to them first of all that the Kingdom of Heaven exists, that all, rich and poor alike, are brothers, and One their Master, He who ascended up on high and led captivity captive, and received gifts for men, the gifts of healing, the gifts of science, the gifts of civilization, the gifts of law, the gifts of order, the gifts of liberty, the gifts of the spirit of love and brotherhood, of fellow-feeling and self-sacrifice, of justice and humility, a spirit fit for a world of redeemed and pardoned men, in which mercy is but justice, and self-sacrifice the truest self-interest; a world, the King and Master of which is One who poured out his own life-blood for the sake of those who hated him, that men should henceforth live not for themselves, but for Him who died and rose again, and ascended up on high and received gifts for men, that the Lord God might dwell among them.

And because all general truths can only be verified in particular instances, verify your general faith in that Christianity which you profess in this particular instance, by doing the duty which lies nearest to you, and *giving, as it is called*, to this Hospital for which I now plead.

Thanks to the spirit and the attainments of the average of English medical men and chaplains, to praise the management of any Hospital which is under their care, is a needless impertinence. Do you find funds, there will be no fear as to their being well employed; and no fear, alas! either of their services being in full demand, while the sanitary state of vast streets of South London, lying close to this Hospital, are in a state in which they are, and in which private cupidity and neglect seem willing to compel them to remain. It is on account of its contiguity to these neglected, destitute, and poisonous localities, that this Hospital seems to me especially valuable. But though situated in a part of London where its presence is especially needed, it has not, from various causes which have arisen from no fault of its own, attracted as much public notice as some other more magnificent foundations; while it possesses one feature, peculiar I believe to it, among our London Hospitals, which seems to me to render it especially deserving of support: I speak of the ward for incurable patients, in which, instead of ending their days in the melancholy wards of a workhouse, or amid those pestilential and crowded dwellings which have perhaps produced their maladies, and which certainly will aggravate them, they may have their heavy years of hopeless suffering softened by a continued supply of constant comforts, and constant medical solicitude, such as the best-conducted workhouse, or the most laborious staff of parish surgeons, and district visitors, ay, not even the benevolence and self-sacrifice of friends and relations, can possibly provide. I beseech you, picture to yourselves the amount of mere physical comfort, not to mention the higher blessings of spiritual teaching and consolation, accruing to some poor tortured cripple, in the wards of this hospital;

compare it with the very brightest lot possible for him in the dwellings of the lower, or even of the middle classes of the metropolis; then recollect that these hospital luxuries, which would be unattainable by him elsewhere, are but a tithe of those which you, in his situation, would consider absolute necessaries, without which a life of suffering, ay, even of health, were intolerable—and do unto others this day, as you would that others should do unto you!

I might have taken some other and more popular method of drawing your attention to this institution. I might have tried to excite your feelings and sympathies by attempts at pathetic or picturesque descriptions of suffering. But the minister of a just God is bound to proclaim that God demands not *sentiment*, but *justice*. The Bible knows nothing of the 'religious sentiments and emotions,' whereof we hear so much talk now-a-days. It speaks of *duty*. 'Beloved, if God so loved us, we *ought* to love one another.'

I might also have attempted to flatter you into giving, by representing this as a '*good work*,' a work of charity and piety, well pleasing to God; a sort of work of Protestant supererogation, fruits of faith which we may show, if we like, up to a certain not very clearly-defined point of benevolence, but the absence of which probably will not seriously affect our eternal salvation, still less our right to call ourselves orthodox, Protestants, churchmen, worthy, kind-hearted, respectable, blameless. The Bible knows nothing of such a religion; it neither coaxes nor flatters, it *commands*. It demands mercy, because mercy is justice; and declares that with what measure we mete to others, it shall be surely measured to us again. If therefore my words shall seem to some here, to be not so much a humble request as a peremptory demand, I cannot help it. I have pleaded the cause of this Hospital on the only solid ground of which I am aware, for doing anything but evil to every one around us who is not a private friend, or a member of one's own family. I ask you to help the poor to their share in the gifts which Christ received for men, because they are His gifts, and neither ours nor any man's. Among these venerable buildings, the signs and witnesses of the Kingdom of God, and the blessings of that Kingdom which for a thousand years have been spreading and growing among us —I ask it of you as citizens of that Kingdom. Prove your brotherhood to the poor by restoring to them a portion of that wealth which, without their labour, you could never have possessed. Prove your brotherhood to them in a thousand ways—in every way—in this way, because at this moment it happens to be the nearest and the most immediate, and because the necessity for it is nearer, more immediate, to judge by the signs of the times, and most of all by their self-satisfied unconsciousness of danger, their loud and shallow self-glorification, than ever it was before. Work while it is called to-day, lest the night come wherein no man can work, but only take his wages.

Again I say, I may seem to some here to have pleaded the cause of this Hospital in too harsh and peremptory a tone. . . And yet I have a ground of hope, in the English love of simple justice, in the noble instances of benevolence and self-sacrifice among the wealthy and educated, which are, thank God! increasing in number daily, as the need of them increases—in these, I say, I have a ground of hope that there are many here to-day who would sooner hear the language of truth than of flattery; who will be more strongly moved toward a righteous deed by being told that it is their duty toward God, their country, and their fellow-citizens, than by any sentimental baits for personal sympathy, or for the love of Pharisaic ostentation.

XIII.

FIRST SERMON ON THE CHOLERA.

Sunday Morning, September 27, 1849.

Psalm x. 5.

God's judgments are from above, out of the sight of the wicked.

WE have just been praying to God to remove from us the cholera, which we call a judgment of God, a chastisement: and God knows we have need enough to do so. But we can hardly expect God to withdraw His chastisement unless we correct the sins for which he chastised us, and therefore unless we find out what particular sins have brought the evil on us. For it is mere cant and hypocrisy, my friends, to tell God, in a general way, that we believe He is punishing us for our sins, and then to avoid carefully confessing any particular sin, and to get angry with any one who tells us boldly *which* sin God is punishing us for. But so goes the world. Every one is ready to say 'Oh! yes, we are all great sinners, miserable sinners!' and then if you charge them with any particular sin, they bridle up and deny *that* sin fiercely enough, and all sins one by one, confessing themselves great sinners, and yet saying that they don't know what sins they have committed. No man really believes himself a sinner, no man really confesses his sins, but the man who can honestly put his finger on *this* sin or *that* sin which he has committed, and is not afraid to confess to God— '*This* sin and *that* sin have I done—*this* bad habit and *that* bad habit have I cherished within me.' Therefore, I say, it is no use for us Englishmen to dream that we can flatter and persuade the great God of Heaven and earth into taking away the cholera from us, unless we find out and confess openly what we have done to bring on the cholera, and unless we repent and bring forth fruits worthy of repentance, by amending our habits on that point, and doing everything for the future which shall not bring on the cholera, but keep it off.

Do not let us believe this time, my friends, in the pitiable, insincere way in which all England believed when the cholera was here sixteen years ago. When they saw human beings dying by thousands of the pestilence, they all got frightened, and proclaimed a Fast, and confessed their sins and promised repentance in a general way. But did they repent of and confess those sins which had caused the cholera? Did they repent of and confess the covetousness, the tyranny, the carelessness, which in most great towns, and in too many villages also, forces the poor to lodge in undrained stifling hovels, unfit for hogs, amid vapours and smells which send forth on every breath the seeds of rickets and consumption, typhus and scarlet fever, and worse and last of all, the cholera? Did they repent of their sin in that?—Not they. Did they repent of the carelessness and laziness and covetousness which sends meat and fish up to all our large towns in a half putrid state—which fills every corner of London and the great cities with slaughter-houses, over-crowded grave-yards, undrained sewers?—Not they. To confess their sins in a general way cost them a few words: to confess and repent of the real particular sins in themselves, was a very different matter; to amend them would have touched vested interests, would have cost money, the Englishman's god; it would have required self-sacrifice of pocket, as well as of time. It would have required manful fighting against the prejudices, the ignorance, the self-conceit, the laziness, the covetousness of the wicked world. So they could not afford to repent and amend of all *that*. And when those great and good men, the Sanitary Commissioners, proved to all England fifteen years ago, that cholera always appeared where fever had appeared, and that both fever and cholera always cling exclusively to those places where there was bad food, bad air, crowded bedrooms, bad drainage and filth—that such were the laws of God and Nature, and always had been; they took no notice of it, because it was the poor rather than the rich who suffered from those causes. So the filth of our great cities was left to ferment in poisonous cesspools, foul ditches and marshes and muds, such as those now killing people by hundreds in the neighbourhood of Plymouth; for one house or sewer that was improved, a hundred more were left just as they were in the first cholera; as soon as the panic of superstitious fear was past, carelessness and indolence returned. Men went back, the covetous man to his covetousness, and the idler to his idleness. And behold! sixteen years are past, and the cholera is as bad as ever among us.

But you will say, perhaps, it is presumptuous to say that Englishmen have brought the cholera on themselves, that it is God's judgment, and that we cannot explain His inscrutable Providence. Ah! my friends, that is a poor excuse and a common one, for leaving a great many sins as they are! When people do not wish to do God's will, it is a very pleasant thing to talk about God's will as something so very deep and unfathomable, that poor human beings cannot be expected to find it

FIRST SERMON ON THE CHOLERA. 181

out. It is an old excuse, and a great favourite with Satan, I have no doubt. Why cannot people find out God's will?—Because they do not *like* to find it out, lest it should shame them and condemn them, and cost them pleasure or money—because their eyes are blinded with covetousness and selfishness, so that they cannot see God's will, even when they *do* look for it, and then they go and cant about God's judgments; while those judgments, as the text says, are far above out of their mammon-blinded and prejudice-blinded sight. What do they mean by that word? Come now, my friends! let us face the question like men. What do you mean really when you call the cholera, or fever, or affliction at all, God's judgment? Do you merely mean that God is punishing you, you don't know for what, and you can't find out for what? but that all which He expects of you is to bear it patiently, and then go and do afterwards just what you did before? Dare any one say that who believes that God is a God of justice, much less a God of love? What would you think of a father who punished his children, and then left them to find out as they could what they were punished for? And yet that is the way people talk of pestilence and of great afflictions, public and private. They are not ashamed to accuse God of a cruelty and an injustice which they would be ashamed to confess themselves!

182 FIRST SERMON ON THE CHOLERA.

How can men, even religious men often, be so blasphemous? Mainly, I think, because they do not really believe in God at all, they only believe about Him—they believe that they ought to believe in Him. They have no living personal faith in God or Christ; they do not know God; they do not know God's character, and what to believe of Him, and what to expect of Him; or what they ought to say of Him; because they do not know, they have not studied, they have not loved the character of Christ, who is the express image and likeness of God. Therefore God's judgments are far away out of their sight; therefore they make themselves a God in their own image and after their own likeness, lazy, capricious, revengeful; therefore they are not afraid or ashamed to say that God sends pestilence into a country without showing that country why it is sent. But another great reason, I believe, why God's judgments in this and other matters are far above out of our sight, is the careless, insincere way of using words which we English have got into, even on the most holy and awful matters. I suppose there never was a nation in the world so diseased through and through with the spirit of cant, as we English are now: except perhaps the old Jews, at the time of our Lord's coming. You hear men talking as if they thought God did not understand English, because they

FIRST SERMON ON THE CHOLERA. 183

cling superstitiously to the letter of the Bible in proportion as they lose its spirit. You hear men taking words into their mouths which might make angels weep and devils tremble, with a coolness and oily, smooth carelessness which shows you that they do not feel the force of what they are saying. You hear them using the words of Scripture, which are in themselves stricter and deeper than all the books of philosophy in the world, in such a loose unscriptural way, that they make them mean anything or nothing. They use the words like parrots, by rote, just because their forefathers used them before them. They will tell you that cholera is a judgment for our sins, 'in a sense,' but if you ask them for what sins, or in what sense, they fly off from that *home* question, and begin mumbling common-places about the inscrutable decrees of Providence, and so on. It is most sad, all this; and most fearful also.

Therefore, I asked you, my friends, what is the meaning of that word judgment? In common talk, people use it rightly enough, but when they begin to talk of God's judgments, they speak as if it merely meant punishments. Now judgment and punishment are two things. When a judge gives judgment, he either acquits or condemns the accused person; he gives the case for the plaintiff, or for the defendant: the punishment of the guilty person, if he be guilty, is a separate thing, pronounced and inflicted afterwards. His judgment, I say, is his *opinion* about the person's guilt, and even so God's judgments are the expression of His opinion about our guilt. But there is this difference between man and God in this matter—a human judge gives his opinion in words, God gives His in *events :* therefore there is no harm for a human judge, when he has told a person why he must punish, to punish him in some way that has nothing to do with his crime—for instance, to send a man to prison because he steals, though it would be far better if criminals could be punished in kind, and if the man who stole could be forced either to make restitution, or work out the price of what he stole in hard labour. For this is God's plan—God always pays sinners back in kind, that He may not merely punish them, but *correct* them; so that by the kind of their punishment, they may know the kind of their sin. God punishes us, as I have often told you, not by His caprice, but by His laws. He does not *break His laws* to harm us; the laws themselves harm us, when we break them and get in their way. It is always so, you will find, with great national afflictions. I believe, when we know more of God and His laws, we shall find it true even in our smallest private sorrows. God is unchangeable; He does not lose His temper, as heathens and superstitious men fancy, to punish us. He does not change His order to punish us. *We* break His order, and the order goes on in spite of us and crushes us: and so we get God's judgment, God's opinion of our breaking His laws. You will find it so almost always in history. If a nation is laid waste by war, it is generally their own fault. They have sinned against the law which God has appointed for nations. They have lost courage and prudence, and trust in God, and fellow-feeling and unity, and they have become cowardly and selfish and split-up into parties, and so they are easily conquered by their own fault, as the Bible tells us the Jews were by the Chaldeans; and their ruin is God's judgment, God's opinion plainly expressed of what He thinks of them for having become cowardly and selfish, and factious and disinterested. So it is with famine again. Famines come by a nation's own fault—they are God's plainly spoken opinion of what *He* thinks of breaking His laws of industry and thrift, by improvidence and bad farming. So when a nation becomes poor and bankrupt, it is its own fault; that nation has broken the laws of political economy which God has appointed for nations, and its ruin is God's judgment, God's plain-spoken opinion again of the sins of extravagance, idleness, and reckless speculation.

186 FIRST SERMON ON THE CHOLERA.

So with pestilence and cholera. They come only because we break God's laws; as the wise poet well says,

> 'Voices from the depths *of Nature* borne
> Which vengeance on the guilty head proclaim.'

—' Of nature ;' of the order and constitution which God has made for this world we live in, and which if we break them, though God in his mercy so orders the world that punishment comes but seldom even to our worst offences, yet surely do bring punishment sooner or later if broken, in the common course of nature. Yes, my friends, as surely and naturally as drunkenness punishes itself by a shaking hand and a bloated body, so does filth avenge itself by pestilence. Fever and cholera, as you would expect them to be, are the expression of God's judgment, God's opinion, God's handwriting on the wall against us for our sins of filth and laziness, foul air, foul food, foul drains, foul bed-rooms. Where they are, there is cholera. Where they are not, there is none, and will be none, because they who do not break God's laws, God's laws will not break them. Oh! do not think me harsh, my friends; God knows it is no pleasant thing to have to speak bitter and upbraiding words; but when one travels about this noble land of England, and sees what a blessed place it might be, if we would only do God's will, and what a miserable place it is just because we will not do God's will, it is enough to make one's soul boil over with sorrow and indignation; and then when one considers that other men's faults are one's own fault too, that one has been adding to the heap of sins by one's own laziness, cowardice, ignorance, it is enough to break one's heart—to make one cry with St. Paul, ' Oh wretched man that I am, who shall deliver me from the body of this death ?' Ay, my friends, the state of things in England now is enough to drive an earnest man to despair, if one did not know that all our distresses, and this cholera, like the rest, are indeed *God's* judgments; the judgments and expressed opinions, not of a capricious tyrant, but of a righteous and loving Father, who chastens us just because He loves us, and afflicts us only to teach us his will, which alone is life and happiness. Therefore we may believe that this very cholera is meant to be a blessing; that if we will take the lesson it brings, it will be a blessing to England. God grant that all ranks may take the lesson— that the rich may amend their idleness and neglect, and the poor amend their dirt and stupid ignorance; then our children will have cause to thank God for the cholera, if it teaches us that cleanliness is indeed next to holiness, if it teaches us, rich and poor, to make the workman's home what it ought to be. And believe me, my friends, that day will surely come; and these distresses, sad as they are for the time, are only helping to hasten it —the day when the words of the Hebrew prophets shall be fulfilled, where they speak of a state of comfort and prosperity, and civilization, such as men had never reached in their time—how the wilderness shall blossom like the rose, and there shall be heaps of corn high on the mountain-tops, and the cities shall be green as grass on the earth, instead of being the smoky, stifling, hot-beds of disease which they are now—and how from the city of God streams shall flow for the healing of the nations : strange words, those, and dim; too deep to be explained by any one meaning, or many meanings, such as our small minds can give them; but full of blessed cheering hope. For of whatever they speak, they speak at least of this—of a time when all sorrow and sighing shall be done away, when science and civilization shall go hand in hand with Godliness—when God shall indeed dwell in the hearts of men, and His kingdom shall be fulfilled among them, when 'His ways shall be known upon earth at last, and His saving health among all nations'—of a time when all shall know Him, from the least unto the greatest, and be indeed His children, doing no sin, because they will have given up themselves, their selfishness and cruelty and covetousness, and stupidity and laziness, to be changed and renewed into God's likeness. Then all these distresses and pestilences, which, as I have shown you, come from breaking the will of God, will have passed away like ugly dreams, and all the earth shall be blessed, because all the earth shall at last be fulfilling the words of the Lord's Prayer, and God's will shall be done on earth, even as it is done in heaven. Oh! my friends, have hope. Do you think Christ would have bid us pray for what would never happen? Would He have bid us all to pray that God's will might be done unless He had known surely that God's will would one day be done by men on earth below even as it is done in heaven?

XIV.

SECOND SERMON ON THE CHOLERA.

Exodus xx. 5.

Visiting the sins of the fathers upon the children.

IN my sermon last Sunday I said plainly that cholera, fever, and many more diseases were man's own fault, and that they were God's judgments just because they were man's own fault, because they were God's plain-spoken opinion of the sin of filth and of habits of living unfit for civilized Christian men.

But there is an objection which may arise in some of your minds, and if it has not risen in *your* minds, still it has in other people's often enough; and therefore I will state it plainly, and answer it as far as God shall give me wisdom. For it is well to get to the root of all matters, and of this matter of Pestilence among others; for if we do believe this Pestilence to be God's judgment, then it is a spiritual matter most proper to be spoken of in a place like this church, where men come as spiritual beings to hear that which is profitable for their souls. And it *is* profitable for their souls to consider this matter; for it has to do, as I see, more and more daily with the very deepest truths of the Gospel; and according as we believe the Gospel, and believe really that Jesus Christ is our Saviour and our King, the New Adam, the first-born among many brethren, who has come down to proclaim to us that we are all brothers in Him—in proportion as we believe *that*, I say, shall we act upon this very matter of public cleanliness.

The objection which I mean is this: people say it is very hard and unfair to talk of cholera or fever being people's own fault, when you see persons who are not themselves dirty, and innocent little children, who if they are dirty are only so because they are brought up so, catch the infection and die of it. You cannot say it is their fault. Very true. I did not say it was their fault. I did not say that each particular person takes the infection by his own fault, though I do say that nine out of ten do. And as for little children, of course it is not their fault. But, my friends, it must be some one's fault. No one will say that the world is so ill made that these horrible diseases must come in spite of all man's care. If it was so, plagues, pestilences, and infectious fevers would be just as common now in England, and just as deadly as they were in old times; whereas there is not one infectious fever now in England for ten that there used to be five hundred years ago. In ancient times fevers, agues, plague, small-pox, and other diseases, whose very names we cannot now understand, so completely are they passed away, swept England from one end to the other every few years, killing five people where they now kill one. Those diseases, as I said, have many of them now died out entirely; and those which remain are becoming less and less dangerous every year. And why? Simply because people are becoming more cleanly and civilized in their habits of living; because they are tilling and draining the land every year more and more, instead of leaving it to breed disease, as all uncultivated land does.* It is not merely that doctors are becoming wiser: we ourselves are becoming more reasonable in our way of living. For instance, in large districts both of Scotland and of the English fens, where fever and ague filled the country and swept off hundreds every spring and fall thirty years ago, fever and ague are now almost unknown, simply because the marshes have all been drained in the mean time. So you see that people can prevent these disorders, and therefore it must be some one's fault if they come. Now whose fault is it? You dare not lay the blame on God. And yet you do lay the fault on God if you say that it is no *man's* fault that children die of fever. But I know what the answer to that will be—'We do not accuse God—it is the fault of the fall, Adam's curse which brought death and disease into the world.' That is a common answer, and the very one I want to hear. What? is it just to say, as many do, that all the diseases which ever tormented poor little innocent children all over the world, came from Adam's sinning six thousand years ago, and yet that it is unfair to say that one little child's fever came from his parents' keeping a filthy house a month ago? That is swallowing a camel and straining at a gnat—that God should be just in punishing all mankind for Adam's sin, and yet unjust in punishing one little child for its parents' sin. If the one is just, the other must be just too, I think. If you believe the one, why not believe the other? Why? Because Adam's curse and 'original' sin, as people call it, is a good and pleasant excuse for laying our sins and miseries at Adam's door; but the same rule is not so pleasant in the case of filth and fever, when it lays other people's miseries at our door.

I believe that all the misery in the world sprung from Adam's disobedience and falling from God. 'By one man sin entered into the world, and death by sin, and so death passed on all men, even on those who had not sinned after the likeness of

Adam's transgression.' So says the Bible, and I believe it says so truly. For this is the law of the earth, God's law which He proclaimed in the text. He does visit the sins of the fathers upon the children unto the third and fourth generation of those who hate Him. It is so. You see it around you daily. No one can deny it. Just as death and misery entered into the world by one man, so we see death and misery entering into many a family. A man or woman is a drunkard, or a rogue, or a swearer: how often their children grow up like them! We have all seen that, God knows, in this very parish. How much more in great cities, where boys and girls by thousands—oh, shame that it should be so in a Christian land!—grow up thieves from the breast, and harlots from the cradle. And why? Why are there, as they say, and I am afraid say too truly, in London alone upwards of 10,000 children under sixteen who live by theft and harlotry? Because the parents of these children are as bad as themselves—drunkards, thieves, and worse—and they bring up their children to follow their crimes. If that is not the father's sins being visited on the children, what is?

How often, again, when we see a wild young man, we say, and justly, 'Poor fellow! there are great excuses for him, he has been so badly brought up.' True, but his wildness will ruin him all the same, whether it be his father's fault or his own that he became wild. If he drinks he will ruin his health; if he squanders his money he will grow poor. God's laws cannot stop for him: he is breaking them, and they will avenge themselves on him. You see the same thing everywhere. A man fools away his money, and his innocent children suffer for it. A man ruins his health by debauchery, or a woman hers by laziness or vanity or self-indulgence, and her children grow up weakly and inherit their parent's unhealthiness. How often, again, do we see passionate parents have passionate children, stupid parents stupid children, mean and lying parents mean and lying children; above all, ignorant and dirty parents have ignorant and dirty children. How can they help being so? They cannot keep themselves clean by instinct; they cannot learn without being taught: and so they suffer for their parents' faults. But what is all this except God's visiting the sins of the fathers upon the children? Look again at a whole parish; how far the neglect or the wickedness of one man may make a whole estate miserable. There is one parish in this very union, and the curse of the whole union it is, which will show us that fearfully enough. See, too, how often when a good and generous young man comes into his estate, he finds it so crippled with debts and mortgages by his forefathers' extravagance, that he cannot do the good he would to his tenants, he cannot fulfil his duty as landlord where God has placed him, and so he and the whole estate must suffer for the follies of generations past. If that is not God visiting the sins of the fathers on the children, what is it?

Look again at a whole nation; the rulers of two countries quarrel, or pretend to quarrel, and go to war—and some here know what war is—just because there is some old grudge of a hundred years standing between two countries, or because rulers of whose names the country people, perhaps, never heard, have chosen to fall out, or because their forefathers by cowardice, or laziness, or division, or some other sin, have made the country too weak to defend itself; and for that poor people's property is destroyed, and little infants butchered, and innocent women suffer unspeakable shame. If that is not God visiting the sins of the fathers on the children, what is it?

It is very awful, but so it is. It is the law of this earth, the law of human kind, that the innocent often suffer for other's faults, just as you see them doing in cholera, fever, ague, small-pox, and other diseases which man can prevent if he chooses to take the trouble. There it is. We cannot alter it. Those who will may call God unjust for it.

SECOND SERMON ON THE CHOLERA. 197

Let them first see, whether He is not only most just, but most merciful in making the world so, and no other way. I do not merely mean that whatever God does must be right. That is true, but it is a poor way of getting over the difficulty. God has taught us what is right and wrong, and He will be judged by His own rules. As Abraham said to Him when Sodom was to be destroyed, 'That be far from Thee, to punish the righteous with the wicked. Shall not the Judge of all the earth do right?' Abraham knew what was right, and he expected God not to break that law of right. And we may expect the same of God. And I may be able, I hope, in my sermon next Sunday, to show you that in this matter God does not break the law of right. Nevertheless in the mean time, this is His way of dealing with men. When Sodom was destroyed He brought righteous Lot out of it. But Sodom was destroyed, and in it many a little infant who had never known sin. And just so when Lisbon was swallowed up by an earthquake, ninety years ago, the little children perished as well as the grown people—just as in the Irish famine fever last year, many a doctor and Roman Catholic priest, and Protestant clergyman, caught the fever and died while they were piously attending on the sick. They were acting like righteous men doing their duty at their posts; but God's laws could not turn aside for them. Improvidence, and misrule, which had been working and growing for hundreds of years, had at last brought the famine fever, and even the righteous must perish by it. They had their sins, no doubt, as we all have; but then they were doing God's work bravely and honestly enough, yet the fever could not spare them any more than it could spare the children of the filthy parents, though they had not kept pigsties under their windows, nor cesspools at their doors. It could not spare them any more than it can spare the tenants of the negligent or covetous house-owner, because it is his fault and not theirs that his houses are undrained, overcrowded, destitute, as whole streets in many large towns are, of the commonest decencies of life. It may be the landlord's fault, but the tenants suffer. God visits the sins of the fathers upon the children, and landlords ought to be fathers to their tenants, and must become fathers to them some day, and that soon, unless they intend that the Lord should visit on them all their sins, and their forefathers' also, even unto the third and fourth generation.

For do not fancy that because the innocent suffer with the guilty that therefore the guilty escape. Seldom do they escape in this world, and in the world to come never. The landlord who, as too many do, neglects his cottages till they become mansties, to breed pauperism and disease—the parents whose carelessness and dirt poison their children and neighbours into typhus and cholera— their brother's blood will cry against them out of the ground. It will be required at their hands sooner or later, by Him who beholds iniquity and wrong, and who will not be satisfied in the day of His vengeance by Cain's old answer, 'Am I my brother's keeper?'

We are every one of us our brother's keeper; and if we do not choose to confess that, God will prove it to us in a way that we cannot mistake. A wise man tells a story of a poor Irish widow who came to Liverpool, and no one would take her in or have mercy on her, till, from starvation and bad lodging, as the doctor said, she caught typhus fever, and not only died herself, but gave the infection to the whole street, and seventeen persons died of it. 'See,' says the wise man, 'the poor Irish widow was the Liverpool people's sister after all. She was of the same flesh and blood as they. The fever that killed her killed them, but they would not confess that they were her brothers. They shut their doors upon her, and so there was no way left for her to prove her relationship, but by killing seventeen of them with fever.' A grim jest that, but a true one, like Elijah's jest to the Baal priests on Carmel. A true one, I say, and one that we have all need to lay to heart.

And I do earnestly trust in you that you will lay it to heart. We have had our fair warning here. We have had God's judgment about our cleanliness; His plain spoken opinion about the sanitary state of this parish. We deserve the fever, I am afraid; not a house in which it has appeared but has had some glaring neglect of common cleanliness about it; and if we do not take the warning God will surely some day repeat it. It will repeat itself by the necessary laws of nature; and we shall have the fever among us again, just as the cholera has reappeared in the very towns, and the very streets, where it was seventeen years ago, wherever they have not repented of and amended their filth and negligence. And I say openly, that those who have escaped this time may not escape next. God has made examples, and by no means always of the worst cottages. God's plan is to take one and leave another by way of warning. 'It is expedient that one man should die for the people, and that the whole people perish not' is a great and a sound law, and we must profit by it. So let not those who have escaped the fever fancy that they must needs be without fault. 'Think ye that those sixteen on whom the tower

SECOND SERMON ON THE CHOLERA. 201

of Siloam fell and slew them, were sinners above all those that dwelt at Jerusalem? I say unto you, Nay, but except ye repent, ye shall all likewise perish.'

And I say again, as I said last Sunday, that this is a spiritual question, a Gospel sermon ; for by your conduct in this matter will your faith in the Gospel be proved. If you really believe that Jesus Christ came down from heaven and sacrificed Himself for you, you will be ready to sacrifice yourselves in this matter for those for whom He died ; to sacrifice, without stint, your thought, your time, your money, and your labour. If you really believe that He is the sworn enemy of all misery and disease, you will show yourselves too the sworn enemies of everything that causes misery and disease, and work together like men to put all pestilential filth and damp out of this parish. If you really believe that you are all brothers, equal in the sight of God and Christ, you will do all you can to save your brothers from sickness and the miseries which follow it. If you really believe that your children are God's children, that at baptism God declares your little ones to be His, you will be ready to take any care or trouble, however new or strange it may seem, to keep your children safe from all foul smells, foul food, foul water, and foul air, that they may grow up healthy, hearty, and cleanly, fit to serve God as christened, free, and civilized Englishmen should in this great and awful time, the most wonderful time that the earth has ever seen, into which it has pleased God of His great mercy to let us all be born.

XV.

THIRD SERMON ON THE CHOLERA.

EXODUS xx. 5.

I the Lord thy God am a jealous God, visiting the iniquity of the Fathers upon the children, unto the third and fourth generation of them that hate me.

MANY of you were perhaps surprised and puzzled by my saying in my last sermon that God's visiting the sins of the fathers on the children, and letting the innocent suffer for the guilty, was a blessing and not a curse—a sign of man's honour and redemption, not of his shame and ruin. But the more I have thought of those words, the more glad I am that I spoke them boldly, the more true I find them to be.

I say that there is in them the very deepest and surest ground for hope. 'Yes,' some of you may say, ' to be sure when we see the innocent suffering for the guilty, it is a plain proof that another world must come some day, in which all that unfairness shall be set right.' Well, my friends, it does prove that, but I should be very sorry if it did not prove a great deal more than that—this suffering of the innocent for the guilty. I have no heart to talk to you about the next life, unless I can give you some comfort, some reason for trusting in God in this life. I never saw much good come of it. I never found it do my own soul any good—to be told, ' *This* life and *this* world in which you now live are given up irremediably to misrule and deceit, poverty and pestilence, death and the devil. You cannot expect to set this world right—you must look to the next world. Everything will be set right there.' That sounds fine and resigned ; and there seems to be a great deal of trust in God in it: but, as I think, there is little or none ; and I say so from the fruits I see it bear. If people believe that this world is the devil's world, and only the next world God's, they are easily tempted to say, ' Very well, then, we must serve the devil in this world, and God in the next. We must of course take great care to get our souls saved when we die, that we may go to heaven and live for ever and ever; but as to this world and this life, why we must follow the ways of the world. It is not our fault that they have nothing to do with God. It is not our fault that society and the world are all rotten and accursed ; we found them so when we were born, and we must make the best of a bad matter and sail as the world does, and be covetous

and mean and anxious,—how can we help it?—
and stand on our own rights, and take care of
number one ; and even do what is not quite right
now and then—for how can we help it?—or how
else shall we get on in this poor lost, fallen, sinful
world?'

And so it comes, my friends, that you see people
professing—ay, and believing, Gospel doctrines,
and struggling and reading, and, as they fancy,
praying, morning, noon, and night, to get their own
souls saved,—who yet, if you are to judge by their
conduct, are little better than rogues and heathens;
whose only law of life seems to be the fear of what
people will say of them ; who, like Balaam the son
of Bosor, are trying daily to serve the devil without
God finding it out, worshipping the evil spirit, as
that evil spirit wanted our blessed Lord to do, because they believed his lie, which Christ denied—
that the glory of this world belongs to the evil one ;
and then comforting themselves like Balaam their
father, in the hope that they shall die the death
of the righteous, and their last end be like his.

Now I say, my friends, that this is a lie, and
comes from the father of lies, who tempts every
man, as he tempted our Lord, to believe that the
power and glory of this world are his, that man's
flesh and body, if not his soul, belongs to him. I
say, it is no such thing. The world is God's world.

Man is God's creature, made in God's image, and not in that of a beast or a devil. The kingdom, the power and the glory, *are* God's now. You say so every day in the Lord's Prayer ; believe it. St. James tells you not to curse men, because they are made in the likeness of God now—not *will be* made in God's likeness after they die. Believe that ; do not be afraid of it, strange as it may seem to understand. It is in the Bible ; and you profess to believe that what is in the Bible is true. And I say that this suffering of the innocent for the guilty is a proof of that. If man was not made so that the innocent could suffer for the guilty, he could not have been redeemed at all, for there would have been no use or meaning in Christ's dying for us, the just for the unjust. And more, if the innocent could not suffer for the guilty, we should be like the beasts that perish.

Now, why ? Because just in proportion as any creature is low—I mean in the scale of life—just in that proportion it does without its fellow-creatures, it lives by itself and cares for no other of its kind. A vegetable is a meaner thing than an animal, and one great sign of its being meaner is, that vegetables cannot do each other any good— cannot help each other—cannot even hurt each other, except in a mere mechanical way, by over-growing each other or robbing each other's roots ;

SECOND SERMON ON THE CHOLERA. 207

but what would it matter to a tree if all the other trees in the world were to die? So with wild animals. What matters it to a bird or a beast, whether other birds and beasts are ill off or well off, wise or stupid? Each one takes care of itself —each one shifts for itself. But you will say, 'Bees help each other and depend upon each other for life and death.' True, and for that very reason we look upon bees as being more wise and more wonderful than almost any animals, just because they are so much like us human beings in depending on each other. You will say again, that among dogs, a riotous hound will lead a whole pack wrong —a staunch and well-broken hound will keep a whole pack right; and that dogs do depend upon each other in very wonderful ways. Most true, but that only proves more completely what I want to get at. It is the *tame* dog, which man has taken and broken in, and made to partake more or less of man's wisdom and cunning, who depends on his fellow dogs. The wild dogs in foreign countries, on the other hand, are just as selfish, living every one for himself, as so many foxes might be. And you find this same rule holding as you rise. The more a man is like a wild animal, the more of a *savage* he is, so much more he depends on himself, and not on others—in short, the less civilized he is; for civilized means being a citizen, and learning to live in cities, and to help and depend upon each other. And our common English word 'civil' comes from the same root. A man is 'civil' who feels that he depends upon his neighbours, and his neighbours on him; that they are his fellow-citizens, and that he owes them a duty and a friendship. And, therefore, a man is truly and sincerely civil' just in proportion as he is civilized; in proportion as he is a good citizen, a good Christian—in one word, a *good man*.

Ay, that is what I want to come to, my friends —that word *man*, and what it means. The law of man's life, the constitution and order on which, and on no other, God has made man, is *this*—to depend upon his fellow-men, to be their brothers, in flesh and in spirit; for we are brothers to each other. God made of one blood all nations to dwell on the face of the earth. The same food will feed us all alike. The same cholera will kill us all alike. And we can give the cholera to each other; we can give each other the infection, not merely by our touch and breath, for diseased beasts can do that, but by housing our families and our tenants badly, feeding them badly, draining the land around them badly. This is the secret of the innocent suffering for the guilty, in pestilences, and famines, and disorders, which are handed down from father to child, that we are all of the same blood. This is the reason why Adam's sin infected our whole race. Adam died, and through him all his children have received a certain property of sinfulness and of dying, just as one bee transmits to all his children and future generations the property of making honey, or a lion transmits to all its future generations the property of being a beast of prey. For by sinning and cutting himself off from God Adam gave way to the lower part of him, his flesh, his animal nature, and therefore he died as other animals do. And we his children, who all of us give way to our flesh, to our animal nature, every hour, alas! we die too. And in proportion as we give way to our animal natures we are liable to die; and the less we give way to our animal natures, the less we are liable to die. We have all sinned; we have all become fleshly animal creatures more or less; and therefore we must all die sooner or later. But in proportion as we become Christians, in proportion as we become civilized, in short, in proportion as we become true men, and conquer and keep in order this flesh of ours, and this earth around us, by the teaching of God's spirit, as we were meant to do, just so far will length of life increase and population increase. For while people are savages, that is, while they give themselves up utterly to their own fleshly lusts, and become mere animals like the wild

Indians, they cannot increase in number. They are exposed by their own lusts and ignorance and laziness, to every sort of disease; they turn themselves into beasts of prey, and are continually fighting and destroying each other, so that they seldom or never increase in numbers, and by war, drunkenness, small-pox, fevers, and other diseases too horrible to mention, the fruit of their own lusts, whole tribes of them are swept utterly off the face of the earth. And why? They are like the beasts, and like the beasts they perish. Whereas, just in proportion as any nation lives according to the spirit and not according to the flesh; in proportion as it conquers its own fleshly appetites which tempt it to mere laziness, pleasure, and ignorance, and lives according to the spirit, in industry, cleanliness, chaste marriage, and knowledge, earthly and heavenly, the length of life and the number of the population begin to increase at once, just as they are doing, thank God! in England now; because Englishmen are learning more and more that this earth is God's earth, and that He works it by righteous and infallible laws, and has put them on it to till it and subdue it; that civilization and industry are the cause of Christ and of God; and that without them His kingdom will *not* come, neither will His will be done on earth.

But now comes a very important question. The

beasts are none the worse for giving way to their flesh and being mere animals. They increase and multiply and are happy enough; whereas men, if they give way to their flesh and become animals, become fewer and weaker, and stupider, and viler, and more miserable, generation after generation. Why? Because the animals are meant to be animals, and men are not. Men are meant to be men, and conquer their animal nature by the strength which God gives to their spirits. And as long as they do not do so; as long as they remain savage, sottish, ignorant, they are living in a lie, in a diseased wrong state, just as God did *not* mean them to live; and therefore they perish; therefore these fevers and agues, and choleras, war, starvation, tyranny, and all the ills which flesh is heir to, crush them down. Therefore they are at the mercy of the earth beneath their feet, and the skies above their head; at the mercy of rain and cold; at the mercy of each other's selfishness, laziness, stupidity, cruelty; in short, at the mercy of the brute material earth, and their own fleshly lusts and the fleshly lusts of others, because they love to walk after the flesh and not after the spirit— because they like the likeness of the old Adam who is of the earth earthy, better than that of the new Adam who is the Lord from Heaven—because they like to be animals, when Christ has made

212 THIRD SERMON ON THE CHOLERA.

them in his own image, and redeemed them with His own blood, and taught them with His own example, and made them men. He who will be a man, let him believe that he is redeemed by Christ and must be like Christ in everything he says and does. If he would carry that out, if he would live perfectly by faith in God, if he would do God's will utterly and in all things, he would soon find that those glorious old words still stood true—'Thou shalt not be afraid of the arrow by night, nor of the pestilence which walketh in the noonday: a thousand shall fall at thy side, and ten thousand at thy right hand, but it shall not come nigh thee.' For such a man would know how to defend himself against evil; God would teach him, not only to defend himself, but to defend those around him. He would be like his Lord and Master, a fountain of wisdom and healing and safety to all his neighbours. We might any one of us be that. It is every one's fault more or less that he is not. Each of us who is educated, civilized, converted to the knowledge and love of God, it is his sin and shame that he is *not* that. Above all, it is the clergyman's sin and shame that he is not. Ay, believe me, when I blame you, I blame myself ten thousand times more. I believe there is many a sin and sorrow from which I might have saved you here, if I had dealt with you more as a man should deal who believes that you and I are brothers, made in the same image of God, redeemed by the same blood of Christ. And I believe that I shall be punished for every neglect of you for which I have been ever guilty. I believe it, and I thank God for it; for I do not see how a clergyman, or any one else, can learn his duty, except by God's judging him, and punishing him, and setting his sins before his face.

Yes, my friends, it is good for us to be afflicted, good for us to suffer anything which will teach us this great truth, that we are our brother's keepers; that we are all one family, and that where one of the members suffers, all the other members suffer with it; and that if one of the members has cause to rejoice, all the others will have cause to rejoice with it. A blessed thing to know, is that—though whether we know it or not, we shall find it true. If we give way to our animal nature, and try to live as the beasts do, each one caring for his own selfish pleasure—still we shall find out that we cannot do it. We shall find out, as those Liverpool people did with the Irish widow, that our fellow-men *are* our brothers—that what hurts them will be sure in some strange indirect way to hurt us. Our brothers here have had the fever, and we have escaped: but we have felt the fruits of it, in our purses—in fear, and anxiety, and distress, and trouble—we have found out that they could not have the fever without our suffering for it, more or less. You see we are one family—we men and women; and our relationship will assert itself in spite of our forgetfulness, and our selfishness. How much better to claim our brotherhood with each other, and to act upon it—to live as brothers indeed. That would be to make it a blessing, and not a curse; for as I said before, just because it is in our power to injure each other, therefore it is in our power to help each other. God has bound us together for good and for evil, for better for worse. Oh! let it be henceforward in this parish for better, and not for worse. Oh! every one of you, whether you be rich or poor, farmer or labourer, man or woman, do not be ashamed to own yourselves to be brothers and sisters, members of one family, which as it all fell together in the old Adam, so it has all risen together in the new Adam, Jesus Christ. There is no respect of persons with God. We are all equal in His sight. He knows no difference among men, except the difference which God's Spirit gives, in proportion as a man listens to the teaching of that Spirit—rank in godliness and true manhood. Oh! believe that—believe that because you owe an infinite debt to Christ and to God, His Father and your Father, therefore you owe an infinite debt to your neighbours, members of Christ and children of God just as you are—a debt of love, help, care, which you *can* pay, just because you are members of one family; for because you are members of one family, for that very reason every good deed you do for a neighbour, does not stop with that neighbour, but goes on breeding and spreading, and growing and growing, for aught we know, for ever. Just as each selfish deed we do, each bitter word we speak, each foul example we set, may go on spreading from mouth to mouth, from heart to heart, from parent to child, till we may injure generations yet unborn; so each noble and self-sacrificing deed we do, each wise and loving word we speak, each example we set of industry and courage, of faith in God, and care for men, may and will spread on from heart to heart, and mouth to mouth, and teach others to do and be the like; till people miles away, who never heard of our names, may have cause to bless us for ever and ever. This is one and only one of the glorious fruits of our being one family. This is one and only one of the reasons which make me say, that it was a good thing mankind was so made, that the innocent suffer for the guilty. For just as the innocent are injured by the guilty in this world, even so are the guilty preserved, and converted, and brought back again by the innocent. Just as the sins of the fathers are visited on the children, so is the righteousness of the fathers a blessing to the children; else, says St. Paul, our children would be unclean, but now they are holy. For the promises of God are not only to us, but to our children, even to as many as the Lord our God shall call. And thus each generation, by growing in virtue and wisdom and the knowledge of God, will help forward all the generations which follow it to fuller light and peace and safety; and each parent in trying to live like a Christian man himself, will make it easier for his children to live like Christians after him. And this rule applies even in the things which we are too apt to fancy unimportant — every house kept really clean, every family brought up in habits of neatness and order, every acre of foul land drained, every new improvement in agriculture and manufactures or medicine, is a clear gain to all mankind, a good example set which is sure sooner or later to find followers, perhaps among generations yet unborn, and in countries of which we never heard the name.

Was I not right then in saying that this earth is not the devil's earth at all, but a right good earth of God's making and ruling, wherein no good deed will perish fruitless, but every man's works will follow him—a right good earth, governed by a righteous Father, who, as the Psalm says, 'is merciful,' just 'because He rewards every man according to his work.'

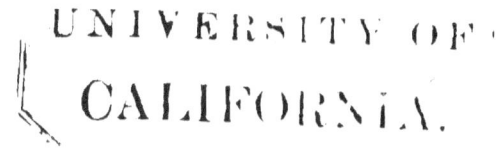

XVI.

ON THE DAY OF THANKSGIVING.

Nov. 15th, 1849.

LUKE vii. 16.
God hath visited his people.

WE are assembled this day to thank God solemnly for the passing away of the cholera from England; and we must surely not forget to thank Him at the same time for the passing away of the fever, which has caused so much expense, sorrow, and death among us. Now I wish to say a very few words to you on this same matter, to show you not only *how* to be thankful to God, but what to be thankful for. You may say, It is easy enough for us to know what to thank God for in this case. We come to thank Him, as we have just said in the public prayers, for having withdrawn this heavy visitation from us. If so, my friends, what we shall thank him for depends on what we mean by talking of a visitation from God.

Now I do not know what people may think in this parish, but I suspect that very many all over England do *not* know what to thank God for just now;

and are altogether thanking him for the wrong thing —for a thing which, very happily for them He has *not* done for them, and which, if He had done it for them, would have been worse for them than all the evil which ever happened to them from their youth up until now. To be plain then, many, I am afraid, are thanking God for having gone away and left them. While the cholera was here, they said that God was visiting them; and now that the cholera is over, they consider that God's visit is over too, and are joyful and light of heart thereat. If God's visit is over, my friends, and He is gone away from us; if He is not just as near us now as He was in the height of the cholera, the best thing we can do is to turn to Him with fasting, and weeping, and mourning, and roll ourselves in the dust, and instead of thanking our Father for going away, pray to Him, of His infinite mercy, to condescend to come back again and visit us, even though, as superstitious and ignorant men believe, God's visiting us were sure to bring cholera, or plague, or pestilence, or famine, or some other misery. For I read, that in His presence is life and not death—at His right hand is fulness of joy, and not tribulation and mourning and woe; but if not, it were better to be with God in everlasting agony, than to be in everlasting happiness without God.

ON THE DAY OF THANKSGIVING. 219

Here is a strange confusion!—people talking one moment like St. Paul himself, desiring to be with Christ and God for ever, and then in the same breath talking like the Gadarenes of old, when, after Christ had visited them, and judged their sins by driving their unlawful herd of swine into the sea, they answered by beseeching Him to depart out of their coasts.

Why is this confusion?—Because people do not take the trouble to read their Bibles; because they bring their own loose, careless, cant notions with them when they open their Bibles, and settle beforehand what the Bible is to tell them, and then pick and twist texts till they make them mean just what they like and no more. There is no folly, or filth, or tyranny, or blasphemy, which men have not defended out of the Bible by twisting it in this way. The Bible is better written than that, my friends. He that runs may read, if he has sense to read. The wayfaring man, though simple, shall make no such mistake therein, if he has God's Spirit in him, —the spirit of faith, which believes that the Bible is God's message to men—the humble spirit, which is willing to listen to that message, however strange or new it may seem to him—the earnest spirit, which reads the Bible really to know what a man shall do to be saved. Look at your Bibles thus, my friends, about this matter. Read all the texts which speak of God's visiting and God's visitation, and you will find all the confusion and strangeness vanish away. For see! The Bible talks of the Lord visiting people in his wrath—visiting them for their sins—visiting them with sore plagues and punishments, about forty times. But the Bible speaks very nearly as often of God's visiting people to bring them blessings and not punishments. The Bible says God visited Sarah and Hannah to give them what they most desired—children. God visited the people of Israel in Egypt to deliver them out of slavery. In the book of Ruth we read how the Lord visited His people in giving them bread. The Psalmist, in the captivity at Babylon, *prays* God to visit him with His salvation. The Prophet Jeremiah says that it was a sign of God's anger against the Jews that He had *not* visited them; and the prophets promised again and again to their countrymen, how, after their seventy years' captivity in Babylon, the Lord would visit them, and what for?—To bring them back into their own land with joy, and heap them with every blessing—peace and wealth, freedom and righteousness. So it is in the New Testament too. Zacharias praised God, 'Blessed be the Lord God of Israel, for He hath visited and redeemed His people; through the tender mercy of our God, whereby the day-spring from on high hath visited us.' And that was the reason why I chose Luke vii. 16, for my text—only because it is an example of the same thing. The people, it says, praised God, saying, 'A great Prophet is risen up among us, and God has visited his people.' And in the 14th of Acts we read how God visited the Gentiles, not to punish them, but to take out of them a people for His name, namely, Cornelius and his household. And lastly, St. Peter tells Christian people to glorify God in the day of visitation, as I tell you now—whether His visitation comes in the shape of cholera, or fever, or agricultural distress; or whether it comes in the shape of sanitary reform, and plenty of work, and activity in commerce; whether it seems to you good or evil, glorify God for it. Thank Him for it. Bless Him for it. Whether His visitation brings joy or sorrow, it surely brings a blessing with it. Whether God visits in wrath or in love, still God visits. God shows that He lives; God shows us that He has not forgotten us; God shows us that He is near us. Christ shows us that His words are true, 'Lo, I am with you always, even to the end of the world.'

That is a hard lesson to learn and practise, though not a very difficult one to understand. I will try now to make you understand it—God alone can teach you to practise it. I pray and hope, and I believe too, that He will—that these very hard times are meant to teach people *really* to believe in God and Jesus Christ, and that they *will* teach people. God knows we need, and thanks be to Him that He *does* know that we need, to be taught to believe in Him. Nothing shows it to me more plainly than the way we talk about God's visitations, as if God was usually away from us, and came to us only just now and then—only on extraordinary occasions. People have gross, heathen, fleshly, materialist notions of God's visitations, as if He was some great earthly king who now and then made a journey about his dominions from place to place, rewarding some and punishing others. God is not in any place, my friends. God is a Spirit. The heaven and the heaven of heavens could not contain Him if He wanted a place to be in, as, glory be to His name, He does not. If He is near us or far from us, it is not that He is near or far from our bodies, as the Queen might be nearer to us in London than in Scotland, which is most people's notion of God's nearness. He is near, not our bodies, but our spirits, our souls, our hearts, our thoughts—as it is written, 'The kingdom of God is *within* you.' Do not fancy that when the cholera was in India, God was nearer

India than He was to England, and that as the cholera crawled nearer and nearer, God came nearer and nearer too; and that now the cholera is gone away somewhere or other, God is gone away somewhere or other too, to leave us to our own inventions. God forbid a thousand times! as St. Paul says, 'He is not far from any one of us.' 'In Him we live and move and have our being,' cholera or none. Do you think Christ, the King of the earth, is gone away either—that while things go on rightly, and governments, and clergy, and people do right, Christ is there then, filling them all with His Spirit and guiding them all to their duty; but that when evil times come, and rulers are idle, and clergy dumb dogs, and the rich tyrannous, and the poor profligate, and men are crying for work and cannot get it, and every man's hand is against his fellow, and no one knows what to do or think; and on earth is distress of nations with perplexity, men's hearts failing them for fear, and for dread of those things which are coming on the earth—do you think that in such times as those, Christ is the least further off from us than He was at the best of times?—The least further off from us now than He was from the apostles at the first Whitsuntide? God forbid!—God forbid a thousand times! He has promised Himself, He that is faithful and true,

He that will never deny Himself, though men deny Him, and say He is not here, because their eyes are blinded with love of the world, and covetousness and bigotry, and dread lest He, their Master, should come and find them beating the men-servants and maid-servants, and eating and drinking with the drunken in the high places of the earth, and saying, 'Tush! God hath forgotten it'—Ay, though men have forgotten Him thus, and—worse than thus, yet He hath said it—'Lo, I am with you always, even unto the end of the world.' Why, evil times are the very times of which Christ used to speak as the 'days of the Lord,' and the 'days of the Son of man.'—Times when we hear of wars and rumours of wars, and on earth distress of nations with perplexity—what does He tell men to do in them? To go whining about, and say that Christ has left His church? No! 'Then,' He says, 'when all these things come to pass, then rejoice and lift up your heads, for your redemption draweth nigh.'

And yet the Scripture does most certainly speak of the Lord's coming out of His place to visit—of the Son of Man coming, and not coming to men—of His visiting us at one time and not at another. How does that agree with what I have just said? My dear friends, we shall see that it agrees perfectly with what I have said, if we will only just remember that we are not beasts, but men. It may seem a strange thing to have to remind people of, but it is just what they are always forgetting. My friends, we are not animals, we are not spiders to do nothing but spin, or birds only to build nests for ourselves, much less swine to do nothing but dig after roots and fruits, and get what we can out of the clods of the ground. We are the children of the Most High God; we have immortal souls within us; nay, more, we are our souls: our bodies are our husk—our shell—our clothes—our house—changing day by day, and year by year upon us, one day to drop off us till the Resurrection. But *we* are *our souls*, and when God visits, it is our souls He visits, not merely our bodies. There is the whole secret. People forget God, and therefore they are glad to fancy that He has forgotten them, and has nothing to do with this world of His which they are misusing for their own selfish ends; and then God in His mercy visits them. He knocks at the door of their hearts, saying, 'See! I was close to you all the while.' He forces them to see Him and to confess that He is there whether they choose or not. God is not away from the world. He is away from people's hearts, because He has given people free wills, and with free wills the power of keeping Him out of their hearts or letting Him in. And when God visits He forces Himself on our attention. He knocks at the door of our hard hearts so loudly and sharply that He forces all to confess that He is there—all who are not utterly reprobate and spiritually dead. In blessings as well as in curses, God knocks at our hearts. By sudden good fortune, as well as by sudden mishap; by a great deliverance from enemies, by an abundant harvest, as well as by famine and pestilence. Therefore this cholera has been a true visitation of God. The poor had fancied that they might be as dirty, the rich had fancied that they might be as careless, as they chose; in short, that they might break God's laws of cleanliness and brotherly care without His troubling Himself about the matter. And lo! He has visited us; and shown us that He does care about the matter by taking it into His own hands with a vengeance. He who cannot see God's hand in the cholera must be as blind—as blind as who?—as blind as he that cannot see God's hand when there is no cholera; as blind as he who cannot see God's hand in every meal he eats, and every breath he draws; for that man is stone blind—he can be no blinder. The cholera came; every one ought to see that it did not come by blind chance, but by the will of some wise and righteous Person; for in the first place God gave us fair warning. The cholera came from India at a steady pace. We knew to a month when it would arrive here. And it came, too, by no blind necessity, as if it was forced to take people whether it liked or not. Just as it was in the fever here, so it was in the cholera, 'One shall be taken and another left.' It took one of a street and left another; took one person in a family and left another: it took the rich man who fancied he was safe, as well as the poor man who did not care whether he was safe or not. The respectable man walking home to his comfortable house, passed by some untrapped drain, and then poisonous gas struck him and he died. The rich physician who had been curing others, could not save himself from the poison of the crowded graveyard which had been allowed to remain at the back of his house. By all sorts of strange and unfathomable judgments the cholera showed itself to be working, not by a blind necessity, but at the will of a thinking Person, of a living God, whose ways are not as our own ways, and His paths are in the great deep. And yet the cholera showed—and this is what I want to make you feel—that it was working at the will of the same God in whom we live and move and have our being, who sends the food we eat, the water in which we wash, the air we breathe, and who has ordained for all these things natural laws, according to which they work, and which He never breaks, nor allows us to break them. For every case of cholera could be traced to some breaking of these laws—foul air—foul food—foul water, or careless and dirty contact with infected persons; so that by this God showed that He and not chance ruled the world, and that he was indeed the living and willing God. He showed at the same time that He was the wise God of order and of law; and that gas and earth, wind and vapour, fulfil His word, without His having to break His laws, or visit us by moving, as people fancy, out of a Heaven where He was, down to an earth, where He was not.

But, lastly, remember what I told you before, that the cholera being a visitation means that God, by it, has been visiting our hearts, knocking loudly at them that He may awaken us, and teach us a lesson. And be sure that in the cholera, and this our own parish fever, there is a lesson for each and every one of us if we will learn it. To the simple poor man, first and foremost, God means by the cholera to teach the simple lesson of cleanliness; to the house-owner He means to teach that each man is his brother's keeper, and responsible for his property not being a nest of disease; to rulers it is intended to teach the lesson that God's laws cannot be put off to suit their laziness, cowardice, or party squabbles. But beside that, to each person, be sure such a visitation as this brings some private lesson. Perhaps it has taught many a widow that she has a Friend stronger and more loving than even the husband whom she has lost by the pestilence—the God of the widow and the fatherless. Perhaps it has taught many a strong man not to trust in his strength and his youth, but in the God who gave them to him. Perhaps it has taught many a man, too, who has expected public authorities to do everything for him, 'not to put his trust in princes, nor in any child of man, for there is no help in them,' but to hear God's advice, 'Help thyself and God will help thee.' Perhaps it has stirred up many a benevolent man to find out fresh means for rooting out the miseries of society. Perhaps it has taught many a philosopher new deep truths about the laws of God's world, which may enable him to enlighten and comfort ages yet unborn. Perhaps it has awakened many a slumbering heart, and brought many a careless sinner (for the first time in his life) face to face with God and his own sins. God's judgments are manifold; they are meant to work in different ways on different hearts. But oh! believe and be sure that they are meant to work upon all hearts—that they are! not the punishments of a capricious tyrant, but the rod of a loving Father, who is trying to drive us home into His fold, when gentle entreaties and kind deeds have failed to allure us home. Oh ! my friends, if you wish really to thank God for having preserved you from these pestilences, show your thankfulness by learning the lesson which they bring. God's love has spoken of each and every one of us in the cholera. Be sure He has spoken so harshly only because a gentler tone of voice would have had no effect upon us. Thank Him for His severity. Thank Him for the cholera, the fever. Thank Him for anything which will awaken us to hear the Word of the Lord. But till you have learnt the lessons which these visitations are meant to teach you, there is no use thanking Him for taking them away. And therefore I beseech you solemnly, each and all, before you leave this church, now to pray to God to show you what lesson He means to teach you by this past awful visitation, and also by sparing you and me who are here present, not merely from cholera and fever, but from a thousand mishaps and evils, which we have deserved, and from which only His goodness has kept us. O may God stir up your hearts to ask advice of Him this day ; and may He in His great mercy so teach us all His will on this day of joy, that we may not need to have it taught us hereafter on some day of sorrow.

XVII.

THE COVENANT.

PSALM CXXXV. 4, 5, 6.

The Lord hath chosen Jacob unto himself, and Israel for his own possession. For I know that the Lord is great, and that our Lord is above all gods. Whatsoever the Lord pleased, that did he in heaven and earth, and in the sea, and in all deep places.

WERE you ever puzzled to find out why the Psalms are read every Sunday in Church, more read, indeed, than any other part of the Bible? If any of you say, No, I shall not think you the wiser. It is very easy not to be puzzled with a deep matter, if one never thinks about it at all. But when a man sets his mind to work seriously, to try to understand what he hears and sees around him, then he will be puzzled, and no shame to him; for he will find things every day of his life which will require years of thought to understand, ay, things which, though we see and know that they are true, and can use and profit by them, we can never understand at all, at least in this life.

But I do not think that God meant it to be so

with these Psalms. He meant the Bible for a poor man's book : and therefore the men who wrote the Bible were almost all of them poor men, at least at one time or other of their life; and therefore we may expect that they would write as poor men would write, and such things as poor men may understand, if they are fairly and simply explained. Therefore I do not think you need be puzzled long to find out why these Psalms are read every Sunday. For the men who wrote them had God's spirit with them; and God's spirit is the spirit in which God made and governs this world, and just as God cannot change, so God's spirit cannot change; and therefore the rules and laws according to which the world runs on cannot change; and therefore these rules about God's government of the world, which God's spirit taught the old Hebrew Psalmists, are the very same rules by which He governs it now; and therefore all the rules in these Psalms, making allowance for the difference of circumstances, have just as much to do with France, and Germany, and England now, as they had with the Jews, and the Canaanites, and the Babylonians then.

St. Paul tells us so. He tells us that all that happened to the old Jews was written as an example to Christians, to the intent that they might

THE COVENANT. 233

not sin as the Jews did, and so (God's laws and ways being the same now as they) be punished as the Jews were. Moreover, St. Paul says, that Christians now are just as much God's chosen people as the Jews were. God told the Jews that they were to be a nation of kings and priests to Him. And St. John opens the Revelations by saying, 'Unto him that loved us and washed us from our sins in His own blood, and hath made us kings and priests unto God and His Father, to Him be glory.' St. Paul tells the Ephesians, who had not a drop of Jewish blood in their veins, that through Jesus Christ both Jews and Gentiles had 'access by one spirit unto the Father. Now therefore,' he goes on, ' ye are no more strangers and foreigners, but fellow-citizens with the saints, and of the household of God.' In fact, he tells the Christians of every country to which he writes, that all the promises which God made to the Jews belonged to them just as much, that there was no more any difference between Jew and Gentile, that the Lord Jesus Christ was just as really among them, and with them, ruling and helping each people in their own country, as He was in Jerusalem when Isaiah saw His glory filling the Temple, and when Zion was called the place of His inheritance. Indeed, the Lord Jesus said the same thing Himself, for He said that all power was given to Him in heaven and earth; that He was with His churches (that is, with all companies of Christian people, such as England) even to the end of the world; that wherever two or three were gathered together in His name, He would be in the midst of them; and if those blessed words and good news be true, we Englishmen have a right to believe firmly that we belong to Him just as much as the old Jews did; and when we read these Psalms, to take every word of their good news—and their warnings also, to ourselves, and to our own land of England. And when we read in the text, that the Lord chose Jacob unto himself and Israel for his own possession, we have a right to say, 'And the Lord has chosen also England unto himself, and this favoured land of Britain for his own possession.' When we say in the Psalm, 'The Lord did what He pleased in heaven, and earth, and sea,' to educate and deliver the people of the Jews, we have a right to say just as boldly —'And so He has done for England, for us, and for our forefathers.'

This then is the reason, the chief reason, why these Psalms are appointed to be read every Sunday in Church, and every morning and evening where there is daily service—to teach us that the

Lord takes care not only of one man's soul here, and another woman's soul there, but of the whole country of England; of its wars and its peace; of its laws and government, its progress and its afflictions; of all, in short, that happens to it as a nation, as one body of men, which it is. It must be so, my good friends, else we should be worse off than the old Jews, and not better off, as all the New Testament solemnly assures us a thousand times over that we are.

For in the covenant which God made with the Jews, and in the strange events, good and bad, which He caused to happen to their nation, not only the great saints among them were taken care of, but all classes, and all characters, good and bad, even those who had not wisdom or spiritual life enough to seek God for themselves, still had their share in the good laws, in the teaching and guiding, and in the national blessings which He sent on the whole nation. They had a chance given them of rising, and improving, and prospering, as the rest of their countrymen rose, and improved, and prospered. And when the Lord came to visit Judæa in flesh and blood, we find that He went on the same method. He did not merely go to such men as Philip and Nathaniel, to the holy and elect ones among the Jews, but to the whole people; to the *lost* sheep, as well as to those who were not lost. He did not part the good from the bad before he healed their sicknesses, and fed them with the loaves and fishes. It was enough for Him that they were Jews, citizens of the Jewish nation. God's promises belonged not to one Jew or another, but to the Jewish nation; and even the ignorant and the sinful had a share in the blessings of the covenant, great or small, in proportion as they chose to live as Jews ought, or to forget and deny that they belonged to God's people.

Now, surely the Lord cannot be less merciful now than he was then. He cannot care less for poor orphans, and paupers, and wild untaught creatures, in England now, than he cared for them in Judæa of old. And we see that in fact He does not. For as the wealth of England improves, and the laws improve, and the knowledge of God improves, the condition of all sorts of poor creatures improves too, though they had no share in bringing about the good change. But we are all members of one body, from the Queen on her throne to the tramper under the hedge; and as St. Paul says, 'If one member suffer, all the members suffer with it, and if one member rejoice, all the others' sooner or later 'rejoice with it.' For we, too, are one of the Lord's nations. He has made us one body, with one common language, common laws, common interest, common religion for all; and what He does for one of us, He does for all. He orders all that happens to us; whether it be war or peace, prosperity or dearth, He orders it all; and He orders things so, that they shall work for the good, not merely of a few, but of as many as possible—not merely for His elect, but for those who know Him not. As He has been from the beginning, when He heaped blessings on the stiff-necked and backsliding Israelites—as He was when He endured the cross for a world lying not in obedience, but in wickedness; so is He now; the perfect likeness of His Father, who is no respecter of persons, but causes 'His sun to shine alike on the evil and on the good, and His rain to fall on the just and on the unjust.'

But now, there is one thing against which I have to warn you most solemnly, and especially in such days as these. You may believe my words to your own ruin, or to your own salvation. They are 'The Gospel,' 'The good news of the Kingdom of God,' —that is, the good news that God has condescended to become our King, to govern and guide us, to order all things for our good. But as St. Paul says, the Gospel may be a savour of death unto death, as well as a savour of life unto life. And

I will tell you now; that you have only to do what the Jews just before the coming of our Lord did, and give way to the same thoughts as they, and then, like them, it were better for you that you had never heard of God, and been like the savages, to whom little or no sin is imputed, because they are all but without law. How is this?

As I said before.—Take your covenant privileges as the Pharisees took theirs, and they will turn you into devils while you are fancying yourselves God's especial favourites. Now this was what happened to the Pharisees: they could not help knowing that God had shown especial favour to them; and that He had taught them more about God than He had taught the heathen. But instead of feeling all the more humble and thankful for this, and of remembering day and night that because much had been given to them much would be required of them, they thought more about the honour and glory which God had put on them. They forgot what God had declared, namely, that it was not for their own goodness that He had taught them, for that they were in themselves not a whit better than the heathen around them. They forgot that the reason why He taught them was, that they were to do His work on earth, by witnessing for His name, and telling the heathen that God was their Lord, as well as Lord of the Jews. Now David, and the old Psalmists and Prophets, did not forget this. Their cry is, 'Tell it out among the heathen that the Lord is King.' 'Worship the Son of God, ye kings of the earth, and make your peace with Him lest He be angry.' 'It was in vain,' he told the heathen kings, 'to try to cast away God's government from them, and break His bonds from off them,' for 'The Lord was King, let the nations be never so unquiet.'

But the Jews gradually forgot this, and their daily boast was, That God had nothing to do with the heathen; that He did not care for them, and actually hated them; that they, as it were, had the true God all to themselves for their own private property; and that He had neither love nor mercy, except for them and their proselytes, that is, the few heathens whom they could persuade and entice not to worship the true God after the customs of their own country—that would not have suited the Jews' bigotry and pride—but to turn Jews, and forget their own people among whom they were born, and ape them in everything. And so, as our Lord told them, after compassing sea and land to make one of these proselytes, they only made him after all twice as much the child of hell as themselves. For they could not teach the heathen anything worth knowing about God, when they had forgotten themselves what God was like. They could tell them that there was one God, and not two—but what was the use of that? As St. James says, the devils believe as much as that, and yet the knowledge does not make them holy, but only increases their fear and despair.—And so with these Pharisees. They had forgotten that God was love. They had forgotten that God was merciful. They had forgotten that God was just. And therefore, while they were talking of God and pretending to worship God, they knew nothing of God, and they did not do God's will, and act like God ; for (as we find from the Gospels) they were unjust, tyrannous, proud, conceited, covetous themselves ; and while they were looking down on the poor heathens, these very heathens, the Lord told them, would rise up in judgment against them : for they, knowing little, acted up to the light which they had, better than the Pharisees who knew so much. And so it will be with us, my friends, if we fancy that God's great favours to us are a reason for our priding ourselves on them, and despising Papists and foreigners instead of remembering that just because God has given us so much, He will require more of us. It is true, we do know more of the Gospel than the Papists, who, though they believe in Jesus Christ, worship the Virgin Mary and the Saints, and idols of wood and stone. But if they, who know so little of God's will, yet act faithfully up to what they do know, will they not rise up in judgment against us, who know so much more, if we act worse than they? Instead of despising them, we had better despise ourselves. Instead of fancying that God's love is not over them, and so sinning against God's Holy Spirit, by denying and despising the fruits of God's Holy Spirit in them, we had much better, we Protestants, be repenting of our own sins. We had better pray God to open our eyes to our own want of faith, and want of love, and want of honesty, and want of cleanly and chaste lives; lest God in his anger should let us go on in our evil path, till we fall into the deep darkness of mind of the Pharisees of old. For then, while we were boasting of England as the most Christian nation in the world, we might become the most unchristian, because the most unlike Christ; the most wanting in love and fellow-feeling, and self-sacrifice, and honour, and justice, and honesty;—wanting, in short, in the fruits of the Spirit. And without them there is no use crying, 'We are God's chosen people, He has put His name among us, we alone hate idols, we alone have the pure word of God, and the pure sacraments, and the pure doctrine:' for God may answer us, as He answered the Jews of old, 'Think not to say within yourselves, We have Abraham for our father: Verily, I say unto you, God is able of these stones to raise up children to Abraham.' . . . 'The Kingdom of God shall be taken from you, and given to a nation bringing forth the fruits thereof.' Oh! my friends, let us pray, one and all, that God will come and help us, and with great might succour us, 'that whereas through our sins and wickedness we are sore let and hindered in running the race set before us, God's bountiful grace and mercy may speedily help and deliver us,' and enable us to live faithfully up to the glorious privileges which He has bestowed on us, in calling us 'members of Christ, children of God, and inheritors of the Kingdom of Heaven;' in giving us His Bible, in allowing us to be born into this favoured land of England, in preserving us to this day, in spite of all that we have thought, and said, and done, unworthy of the name of Christians and Englishmen.

And then, we may be certain that God will also fulfil to us the glorious promises which we find in another Psalm:—'If thy children will keep my covenant and my testimonies, which I shall learn them, this land shall be my rest for ever. Here will I dwell, for I have a delight therein. I will bless her victuals with increase, and satisfy her poor with bread. I will deck her priests with health, and her holy people shall rejoice and sing.'

XVIII.

NATIONAL REWARDS AND PUNISHMENTS.

EZEKIEL xx. 32, 33, 38.

And that which cometh into your mind shall not be at all; that ye say, We will be as the heathen, as the families of the countries, to serve wood and stone. As I live, saith the Lord God, surely with a mighty hand, and with a stretched out arm, and with fury poured out, will I rule over you * * * And ye shall know that I am the Lord.

A FATHER has two ways of showing his love to his child,—by caressing it, and by punishing it. His very anger may be a sign of his love, and ought to be. Just because he loves his child, just because the thing he longs most to see is that his child should grow up good, therefore he must be, and ought to be, angry with it when it does wrong. Therefore anger against sin is a part of God's likeness in us; and he who does not hate sin is not like God. For if sin is the worst evil— perhaps the only real evil in the world—and the end of all sin is death and misery, then to indulge people in sin is to show them the very worst of cruelty.

To sit by and see iniquity going on without trying to stop it, is mere laziness. The parent, when his child does wrong, does not show his love to the child by indulging it,—all he shows is, that he himself is carnal and fleshly; that he does not like to take the trouble of punishing it or does not like to give himself the pain of punishing it; that, in short, he had sooner let his child grow up in bad habits, which must lead to its misery and ruin for years and years, if not for ever, than make himself uncomfortable by seeing it uncomfortable for a few minutes. That is not love, but selfishness. True love is as determined to punish the sin as it is to forgive the sinner. Therefore, St. Paul tells us, that we can be angry without sinning; that is, that there is an anger which comes from hatred of sin and love to the sinner. Therefore, Solomon tells us to punish our children when they do wrong, and not to hold our hands for their crying. It is better for them that they should cry a little now, than have long years of shame and sorrow hereafter. Therefore, in all countries which are properly governed, the law punishes in the name of God those who break the laws of God, and punishes them even with death, for certain crimes; because it is expedient that one man die for the people, and that the whole nation perish not.

And this is God's way of dealing with each and

every one of us. This is God's way of dealing with Christian nations, just as it was His way of dealing with the Jews of old. He never allowed the Jews to prosper in sin. He punished them at once and sternly whenever they rebelled against Him; not because He hated them, but because He loved them. His love to them showed itself whenever they went well with Him, in triumphs and blessings;—and when they rebelled against Him, and broke His laws, He showed that very same love to them in plague, and war and famine, and a mighty hand, and fury poured out. His love had not changed,—they had changed; and now the best and only way of showing His love to them, was by making them feel His anger; and the best and only way of being merciful to them, was to show them no indulgence.

Now the wish of the Jews all along, and especially in Ezekiel's time, was to be like the heathen —like the nations round them. They said to themselves, ' These heathen worship idols, and yet prosper very well. Their having gods of wood and stone, and their indulging their passions, and being profligate and filthy, covetous, unjust, and tyrannical, does not prevent their being just as happy as we are,—ay, and a great deal happier. They have no strict law of Moses, as we have, threatening us, and keeping us in awe, and making us uncomfortable, and telling us at every turn, 'Thou shalt not do this pleasant thing, and thou shalt not do that pleasant thing. And yet God does not punish them, as Moses' law says He will punish us. These Assyrians and Babylonians above all— they are stronger than we, and richer, and better clothed, and cleverer; they have horses and chariots, and all sorts of luxuries and comforts which we Jews cannot get. Instead of being like us, in continual trouble from earthquakes, and drought, and famine, and war, attacked, plundered by all the nations round us, one after another, they go on conquering, and spreading, and succeeding in all they lay their hand to. Look at Babylon,' said these foolish Jews perhaps to themselves, 'a few generations ago, it was nothing of a city; and now it is the greatest, richest, and strongest nation in the whole world. God has not punished it for worshipping gods of wood and stone, why should He punish us? These Babylonians have prospered well enough with their gods, why should not we? Perhaps it is these very gods of wood and stone who have helped them to become so great. Why should they not help us? We will worship them, then, and pray to them. We will not give up worshipping our own God, of course, lest we should offend Him: but we will worship Him and the Babylonian idols at the same time; then we shall be sure to be right if we have Jehovah and the idols both on our side.' So said the Jews to themselves. But what did Ezekiel answer them? 'Not so, my foolish countrymen,' said he, 'God will not have it so; He has taught you that these Babylonian idols are nothing and cannot help you; He has taught you that He can and will help you, that He can and will be everything to you; He has taught you that He alone is God, who made heaven and earth, who orders all things therein, who alone gives any people power to get wealth; and He will not have you go back and fall from that for any appearances or arguments whatsoever, because it is true. He has chosen you to witness to these heathen about Him; to declare His name to them, that they may give up their idols and serve the true God, in whom alone is strength. He chose you to be these heathens' teachers, and He will not let you become their scholars. He meant the heathen to copy you, and He will not let you copy them. If He does, in His love and mercy, let these poor heathen prosper in spite of their idols, what is that to you? It is still the Lord who makes them prosper, and not the idols, whether they know it or not. They know no better, and He will not impute sin to them where He has given them no law. But you do know better;—by a thousand mighty signs and wonders and deliverances, the Lord has been teaching you ever since you came up through the Red Sea, that He is all-sufficient for you, that all power is His in heaven and earth. He has promised to you, and sworn to you by Himself, that if you keep His law and walk in His commandments, you shall want no manner of good thing; that you shall have no cause to envy these heathen their riches and prosperity, for the Lord will bless you in house and land, by day and night, at home and abroad, with every blessing that a nation can desire. Moses' law tells you this,—God's prophets have been telling you this,—God's wonderful dealings with you have been telling you this,—that the Lord God is enough for you. And if you, who are meant to be a nation of kings and priests to God, to teach all nations and serve solely Him, fancy that you will be allowed to throw away the high honour which God has put upon you, and lower yourselves to the follies and sins of these heathen round you, you are mistaken. You were meant to be above such folly, you can be above it; and you shall not prosper by serving God and idols at once; you shall not even prosper by serving idols alone. God will visit you with a mighty hand, and with fury poured out, and you shall know that He is the Lord.'

Well, my friends, and what has this to do with

us? This it has to do with us—that if God taught the Jews about Himself, He has taught us still more. If he has shown signs and wonders of His love, and wrought mightily for the Jews, He has wrought far more mightily for us; for He spared not His own Son, but gave Him freely for us. If He promised to teach the Jews, He has promised still more to teach us; for He has promised His Holy Spirit freely to young and old, rich and poor, to as many as ask Him, to guide us into all truth. If he expected the Jews to set an example to all the nations around, He expects us to do so still more. And if He punished the Jews, and drove them back again by shame, and affliction, and disappointment, whenever they went after other gods, and tried to be like the heathen around, and despised their high calling, and their high privileges, He will punish us, and drive us back again still more fiercely, and still more swiftly. God has called us to be a nation of Christians, and He will not let us be a nation of heathens. We are longing to do in these days very much as the Jews did of old; we are all too apt to say to ourselves, 'Of course we must love God, or He might be angry with us; and besides, how else should we get our souls saved? But the old heathen nations, and a great many nations now, and a great many rich and comfortable people in England now, too, get on very well without God, by just worshipping selfishness, and money, and worldly cunning, and why should not we do the same?—why should we not worship God and Mammon at once, and serve God on Sundays, and the selfish ways of the world all the week? Surely then we should be doubly safe; we should have God and the world on our side both at once.'

No, my friends, God will not allow us to succeed on that plan. We are members of His Church, whose head is Jesus, who gave Himself for sinners; whose members are all brothers of His Church, which is held together by self-sacrifice and fellow-help. If we try to be like the heathens, and fancy that we can succeed by selfishness, and cunning, and covetousness, God will not let us fall from the honour which He has put on us, and trample our blessings under foot. He will bring our plans to nought. Whomsoever He may let prosper in sin, He will not let those who have heard the message of His kingdom prosper in it. Whatever nation He may let become great by covetousness, and selfish competing and struggling of man against man, He will not let England grow great by it. He loves her too well to let her fall so, and cast away her high honour of being a Christian nation. By great and sore afflictions, by bringing our cleverest plans to nothing, He will teach us that we cannot worship God and Mammon at once; that the sure riches, either for a man or for a nation, are not money, but righteousness, love, justice, wisdom; that this new idol of selfish competition which men worship now-a-days, and fancy that it is the secret cause of all plenty, and cheapness, and civilization, has no place in the Church of Jesus Christ, who gave up His own life for those who hated Him, and came not to do His own will, but the will of His Father; not to enable men to go to heaven after a life of selfishness here; but by the power of His Spirit,—the spirit of love and fellowship, to sweep all selfishness off the face of God's good earth. By sore trials and afflictions will God in His mercy teach this to England, and to every man in England who is deluded into fancying that he can serve God and selfishness at once, till we learn once more, as our forefathers did of old, that He is the Lord. Because we are His children, God will chasten us; because He receives us, He will scourge us back to Him; because He has prepared for us things such as eye hath not seen, He will not let us fill our bellies with the husks which the swine eat, and like the dumb beasts, snarl and struggle one against the other for a place at His table, as if it were not wide enough for all His creatures, and for ten times as many more, forgetting that He is the giver, and fancying that we are to be the takers, and spoiling the gift itself in our hurry to snatch it out of our neighbours' hands. In one word, God will not give us false prosperity, as the children of the world, the flesh, and the devil, because He wishes to give us real prosperity as the sons of God, in the kingdom of His Son Jesus Christ, who died on the cross for us.

XIX.
THE DELIVERANCE OF JERUSALEM.

2 KINGS xix. 35.

And it came to pass that night, that the angel of the Lord went out, and smote in the camp of the Assyrians an hundred and eighty-five thousand: and when they arose in the morning, behold, they were all dead corpses.

YOU heard read in the first lesson last Sunday afternoon, the threats of the king of Assyria against Jerusalem, and his defiance of the true Lord whose temple stood there. In the first lesson for this morning's service, you heard of king Hezekiah's fear and perplexity; of the Lord's answer to him by Isaiah, and of the great and wonderful destruction of the Assyrian army, of which my text tells you. Of course you have a right to ask, 'This which happened in a foreign country more than two thousand years ago, what has it to do with us?' And of course, my preaching about it will be of no use whatsoever, unless I can show you what it has to do with us; what lesson we English here, in the year 1851, are to draw, from the help which God sent the Jews.

THE DELIVERANCE OF JERUSALEM. 255

But to find out that, we must hear the whole story. Before we can find out why God drove the Assyrians out of Judea, we must find out, it seems to me, why He sent them, or allowed them to come into Judea; and to find out that, we must first see how the Jews were behaving in those times, and what sort of state their country was in; and we must find out, too, what sort of a man this great king of Assyria was, and what sort of thoughts were in his heart.

Now, by the favour of God, we can find out this. You will see, in the first thirty-seven chapters of Isaiah's prophecies, a full account of the ways of the Jews in that time, and the reasons why God allowed so fearful a danger to come upon them. The whole first thirty-five chapters belong to each other, and are, so to speak, a spiritual history of the Jews, and the Assyrians, and all the nations round them for many years. A spiritual history,—that is, not merely a history of what they did, but of what they were, what was in their inmost hearts, and thoughts, and spirits; a spiritual history,—that is, not merely of what they thought they were doing, but of what God saw that they were doing—a history of God's mind about them all. Isaiah had God's spirit on him; and so he saw what was going on round him in the same light in which God saw it, and hated it, or praised it, only according as it was good, and according to the good Spirit of God, or bad, and contrary to that Spirit. So Isaiah's history of his own nation, and the nations around him, was very unlike what they would have written for themselves; just as I am afraid he would write a very different history of England now, from what we should write, if we were set to do it. Now what Isaiah thought of the doings of his countrymen, the Jews, I must tell you in another sermon, next Sunday. It will be enough this morning to speak of the king of Assyria.

These kings of Assyria thought themselves the greatest and strongest beings in the world; they thought that their might was right, and that they might conquer, and ravage, and plunder, and oppress every country round them for thousands of miles, without being punished. They thought that they could overcome the True God of Judea, as they had conquered the empty idols and false gods of Sepharvaim, Hena, and Iva. But Isaiah saw that they were wrong. He told his countrymen, 'These Assyrian kings are strong, but there is a stronger King than they, Jehovah the Lord of all the earth. It is He who has sent them to punish nation after nation, Sennacherib is the rod of Jehovah's anger; but he is a fool after all; for all his cunning, for all his armies, he is a fool rushing on his ruin. He may take Tyre, Damascus, Babylon, Egypt itself, and cast their gods into the fire, for they are no gods, but the work of men's hands, wood and stone; but let him once try his strength against the real living God; let the axe once begin to boast itself against Him that hews therewith; and he will find out that there is one stronger than he, one who has been using him as a tool, and who will crush him like a moth the moment he rebels. His father destroyed Samaria and her idols, but he shall not destroy Jerusalem. He may ravage Ephraim, and punish the gluttony, and drunkenness, and oppression of the great landlords of Bashan; he may bring misery and desolation through the length and breadth of the land: there is reason, and reason but too good for that: but Jerusalem, the place where God's honour dwells, the temple without idols, which is the sign that Jehovah is a living God, against it he shall not cast up a bank, or shoot an arrow into it. 'I know,' said Isaiah, 'what he is saying of himself, this proud king of Assyria: but this is what God says of him, that he is only a puppet, a tool in the hand of God, to punish these wicked nations whom he is conquering one by one, and us Jews among the rest. He, this proud king of Assyria, thinks that he is the chosen favourite of the sun, and the moon, and the stars, whom, in his folly, he worships as gods. He will find out who is the real Lord of the earth; he will find out that this great world is ruled by that very God of Israel whom he despises. He will find that there is something in this earth, of which he fancies himself lord and master, which is too strong for him, which will obey God, and not him. God rules the earth, and God rules Tophet, and the great fire-kingdoms which boil and blaze for ever in the bowels of the earth, and burst up from time to time in earthquakes and burning mountains; and God has ordained that they shall conquer this proud king of Assyria, though we Jews are too weak, and cowardly, and split up into parties by our wickedness, to make a stand against him.' . .

This great eruption, or breaking out of burning mountains, which would destroy the king of Assyria's army, was to happen, Isaiah says, close to Jerusalem, nay, it was to shake Jerusalem itself. Jerusalem was to be brought to great misery by everlasting burnings, as well as by being besieged by the Assyrians; and yet the very shaking of the earth and eruption of fire which was nearly to destroy it, was to be the cause of its deliverance. So Isaiah prophesied, and we cannot doubt his words came true. For this may explain to us the way in which the king of Assyria's army was destroyed. The text says, that when they encamped near Jerusalem the messenger of the Lord went out, and slew in one night 180,000 of them, who were all found dead in the morning. How they were killed we cannot exactly tell, most likely by a stream of poisonous vapour, such as often comes forth out of the ground during earthquakes and eruptions of burning mountains, and kills all men and animals who breathe it. That this was the way that this great army was destroyed I have little doubt, not only on account of what Isaiah says in his prophecies of God's 'sending a blast' upon the king of Assyria, but because it was just like the old lesson which God had been teaching the Jews all along, that the earth, and all in it, was His property, and obeyed Him. For what could teach them that more strongly than to see that the earthquakes and burning mountains, of all things on earth the most awful and most murderous, the very things against which man has no defence, obeyed God; burst forth when He chose, and did His work as he willed? For man can conquer almost everything in the world except these burning mountains and earthquakes. He can sail over the raging sea in his ships; he can till the most barren soils; he can provide against famine, rain, and cold, ay, against the thunder itself: but the earthquakes alone are too strong for him. Against them no cunning or strength of man is of any use. Without warning, they make the solid ground under his feet heave, and reel, and sink, hurling down whole towns in a moment, and burying the inhabitants under the ruins, as an earthquake did in Italy only a month ago. Or they pour forth streams of fire, clouds of dust, brimstone, and poisonous vapour, destroying for miles around the woods and crops, farms and cities, and burying them deep in ashes, as they have done again and again, both in Italy and Iceland, and in South America, even during the last few years. How can man stand against them? What greater warning or lesson to him than they, that God is stronger than man; that the earth is not man's property, and will not obey him, but only the God who made it? Now that was just what God intended to teach the Jews all along; that the earth and heaven belonged to Him and obeyed Him; that they were not to worship the sun and stars, as the Assyrians and Canaanites did, nor the earth and the rivers, as the Egyptians did: but to worship the God who made sun and stars, earth and rivers, and to put their trust in Him to guide all heaven and earth aright; and to make all things, sun, earth, and weather, ay, and the very burning mountains and earthquakes, work together for good for them if they loved God. Therefore it was that God gave His law to Moses on the burning mountain of Sinai, amid thunders, and light-

THE DELIVERANCE OF JERUSALEM. 261

nings, and earthquakes, to show them that the lightnings and the mountains obeyed Him. Therefore it was that the earthquake opened the ground and swallowed up Korah, Dathan, and Abiram, who rebelled against Moses. Therefore it was that God once used an earthquake and eruption to preserve David from his enemies, as we read in the eighteenth Psalm. And all through David's Psalms we find how well he had learnt this great lesson which God had taught him. Again and again we find verses which show that he knew well enough who was the Lord of all the earth.

In Isaiah's time, it seems, God taught the Jews once more the same thing. He taught them, and the proud king of Assyria, once and for all, that He was indeed the Lord—Lord of all nations, and King of kings, and also Lord of the earth, and all that therein is. He taught it to the poor oppressed Jews by that miraculous deliverance. He taught it to the cruel invading king by that miraculous destruction. Just in the height of his glory, after he had conquered almost every nation in the east, and overcome the whole of Judea, except that one small city of Jerusalem, Sennacherib's great army was swept away, he neither knew how nor why, in a single night, and utterly disheartened and abashed, he returned to his own land; and even there he found that the God of

Israel had followed him—that the idols whom he worshipped could not save him from the wrath of that God to whom Assyria, just as much as Jerusalem, belonged. For as he was worshipping in the house of Nisroch his God, his two sons smote him with the sword, and there was an end of all his pride and conquests. . . Now Nisroch was the name of a star—the star which we call the planet Saturn ; and the Assyrians fancied in their folly, that whosoever worshipped any particular star, that star would protect and help him. . . But, alas for the king of Assyria, there was One above who had made the stars, and from whose vengeance the stars could not save him ; and so even while he was worshipping, and praying to, this favourite star of his which could not hear him, he fell dead, a murdered man, and found out too late how true were the great words of Isaiah when he prophesied against him.

Yes, my friends, this is the lesson which the Jews had to learn, and which the king of Assyria had to learn, and which we have to learn also; and which God will, in His great mercy, teach us over and over again by bitter trials whensoever we forget it ; that The Lord is King ; that He is near us, living for ever, all-wise, all-powerful, all-loving ; that those who really trust in Him shall never be confounded ; that those who trust in themselves are trying their paltry strength against the God who made heaven and earth, and will surely find out their own weakness, just when they fancy themselves most successful. So it was in Hezekiah's time; so it is now, hard as it may be to us to believe it. The Lord Jehovah, Jesus Christ, who saved Jerusalem from the Assyrians, He still is king, let the earth be never so unquiet. And all men, or governments, or doctrines, or ways of thinking and behaving, which are contrary to His will, or even pretend that they can do without Him, will as surely come to nought as that great and terrible king of Assyria. Though man be too weak to put them down, Christ is not. Though man neglect to put them down, Christ will not. If man dare not fight on the Lord's side against sin and evil, the Lord's earth will fight for Him. Storm and tempest, blight and famine, earthquakes and burning mountains, will do His work, if nothing else will. As He said Himself, if man stops praising Him, the very stones will cry out, and own Him as their king. Not that the blessed Lord is proud, or selfish, or revengeful; God forbid! He is boundless pity, and love, and mercy. But it is just because He is perfect love and pity that He hates sin, which makes all the misery upon earth. He hates it, and he fights against it for ever; lovingly at first, that He may lead sinners to repentance; for He wills the death

264 THE DELIVERANCE OF JERUSALEM.

of none, but rather that all should come to repentance. But if a man will not turn, He will whet His sword; and then woe to the sinner. Let him be as great as the king of Assyria, he must down. For the Lord will have none guide His world but Himself, because none but He will ever guide it on the right path. Yes—but what a glorious thought, that He will guide it, and us, on that right path. Oh blessed news for all who are in sorrow and perplexity! Whatsoever it is that ails you— and who is there, young or old, rich or poor, who has not their secret ailments at heart?—whatsoever ails you, whatsoever terrifies you, whatsoever tempts you, trust in the same Lord who delivered Jerusalem from the Assyrians, and He will deliver you. He will never suffer you to be tempted above that you are able, but will with the temptation also make a way for you to escape, that you may be able to bear it. This has been His loving way from the beginning, and this will be His way until the day when He wipes away tears from all eyes.

PROFESSION AND PRACTICE.

JEREMIAH V. 2.

Though they say, 'The Lord liveth,' surely they swear falsely.

I SPOKE last Sunday morning of the wonderful way in which the Lord delivered the Jews from the Assyrian army, and I promised to try and explain to you this morning, the reason why the Lord allowed the Assyrians to come into Judea, and ravage the whole country, except the one small city of Jerusalem.

My text is taken from the first lesson, from the book of the prophet Jeremiah. And it, I think, will explain the reason to us.

For though Jeremiah lived more than a hundred years after Isaiah, yet he had much the same message from God to give, and much the same sins round him to rebuke. For the Jews were always, as the Bible calls them, 'a backsliding people;' and, as the years ran on, and they began to forget their great deliverance from the Assyrians, they slid back into the very same wrong state of mind in which they were in Isaiah's time, and for which God punished them by that terrible invasion.

Now, what was this?

One very remarkable thing strikes us at once. That when the Assyrians came into Judea, the Jews were *not* given up to worshipping false gods. On the contrary, we find, both from the book of Kings and the book of Chronicles, that a great reform in religion had taken place among them a few years before. Their king Hezekiah, in the very first year of his reign, removed the high places, and cut down the groves (which are said to have been carved idols meant to represent the stars of heaven), and even broke in pieces the brazen serpent which Moses had made, because the Jews had begun to worship it for an idol. He trusted in the Lord God, and obeyed Him, more than any king of Judah. He restored the worship of the true God in the temple, according to the law of Moses, with such pomp and glory as had never been seen since Solomon's time. And not only did he turn to the true God, but his people also. From the account which we find in Chronicles, they seemed to have joined him in the good work. They offered sin-offerings as a token of the wickedness of which they had been guilty, in leaving the true God for idols; and all other kinds of offerings freely and willingly. 'And Hezekiah rejoiced,

PROFESSION AND PRACTICE. 267

and all the people, that God had prepared the people. Moreover, Hezekiah called all the men in Judea up to Jerusalem, to keep the passover according to the law of Moses,' which they had neglected to do for many years, and the people answered his call and 'came, and kept the feast at Jerusalem seven days, with joy and great gladness, offering peace-offerings, and making confession to the God of their fathers.' 'So there was great joy in Jerusalem ; for since the time of Solomon there was not the like in Jerusalem. Then the priests and the Levites arose, and blessed the people, and their voice was heard, and their prayer came up to the Lord's hóly dwelling, even to heaven.' And when it was all finished, the people went out of their own accord, and destroyed utterly all the idols, and high places, and altars throughout the land, and returned to their houses in peace.

Now does not all this sound very satisfactory and excellent ? What better state of mind could people be in ? What a wonderful reform, and spread of true religion ! The only thing like it, that we know, is the wonderful reform and spread of religion in England in the last sixty years, after all the ungodliness and wickedness that went on from the year 1660 to the time of the French war ; the building of churches, the founding of schools, the spread of Bibles, and tracts, and the wonderful increase of gospel preachers, so that every old man will tell you, that religion is talked about and written about now, a thousand times more than when he was a boy. Indeed, unless a man makes a profession of some sort of religion or other, now-a-days, he can hardly hope to rise in the world, so religious are we English become.

Now let us hear what Isaiah thought of all that wonderful spread of true religion in his time; and then, perhaps, we may see what he would think of ours now, if he were alive. His opinion is sure to be the right one. His rules can never fail, for he was an inspired prophet, and saw things as they are, as God sees them; and therefore his rules will hold good for ever. Let us see what they were.

The first chapter of the book of the prophet Isaiah is called 'The vision of Isaiah, the son of Amoz, which he saw concerning Judah and Jerusalem, in the days of Uzziah, Jotham, Ahaz, and Hezekiah.' Now this is one prophecy by itself, in the shape of a poem; for in the old Hebrew it is written in regular verses. The second chapter begins with another heading, and is the beginning of a different poem; so that this first chapter is, as it were, a summing up of all that he is going to say afterwards; a short account of the state of the Jews for more than forty years. And what is more, this first chapter of Isaiah must have been written in the reign of Hezekiah, in those very religious days of which I was just speaking; for it says that the country was desolate, and Jerusalem alone left. And this never happened during Isaiah's lifetime, till the fourteenth year of Hezekiah, that is, till this great spread of the true religion had been going on for thirteen years. Now what was Isaiah's vision? What did he, being taught by God's Spirit, *see* was God's opinion of these religious Jews: Listen, my friends, and take it solemnly to heart!—

'Hear the word of the Lord, ye rulers of Sodom; give ear unto the law of our God, ye people of Gomorrah. To what purpose is the multitude of your sacrifices unto me? saith the Lord: I am full of the burnt offerings of rams, and the fat of fed beasts: and I delight not in the blood of bullocks, or of lambs, or of he-goats. When ye come to appear before me, who hath required this at your hand, to tread my courts? Bring no more vain oblations; incense is an abomination unto me; the new moons and Sabbaths, the calling of assemblies, I cannot away with; it is iniquity, even the solemn meeting. Your new moons and your appointed feasts my soul hateth: they are a trouble unto me; I am weary to bear them. And when ye spread forth your hands, I will hide mine eyes from you; yea, when ye make many prayers, I

will not hear: your hands are full of blood. Wash you, make you clean; put away the evil of your doings from before mine eyes; cease to do evil; learn to do well, seek judgment, relieve the oppressed, judge the fatherless, plead for the widow.
. . . How is the faithful city become an harlot! it was full of judgment; righteousness lodged in it; but now murderers. Thy silver is become dross, thy wine mixed with water; thy princes are rebellious, and companions of thieves; every one loveth gifts, and followeth after rewards: they judge not the fatherless, neither doth the cause of the widow come unto them. Therefore saith the Lord, the Lord of hosts, the mighty one of Israel, Ah, I will ease me of mine adversaries, and avenge me of mine enemies.' . . .

Again, I say, my friends, listen to it, and take it solemnly to heart! That is God's opinion of religion, even the truest and soundest in worship and doctrine, when it is without godliness, without holiness; when it goes hand in hand with injustice, and covetousness, and falsehood, and cheating, and oppression, and neglect of the poor, and keeping company with the wicked, because it is profitable; in short, when it is like too much of the religion which we see around us in the world at this day.

Yes—it was of no use holding to the letter of the law while they forgot its spirit. God had commanded church-going, and woe to those, then or now, who neglect it. Yet the Lord asks, 'Who hath required this at your hands, to tread my courts? . . . He had commanded the Sabbath-day to be kept holy; and woe to those, then or now, who neglect it. Yet He says, 'Your sabbaths I cannot away with; it is iniquity, even the solemn meeting.' The Lord had appointed feasts: and yet He says that His soul hated them; they were a trouble to Him; He was weary to bear them. The Lord had commanded prayer; and woe to those, then or now, in England, as in Judea, who neglect to pray. And yet He says, 'When ye spread forth your hands, I will hide mine eyes from you; yea, when ye make many prayers, I will not hear.' And why?—He himself condescends to tell them the reason, which they ought to have known for themselves; 'Because,' He says, 'your hands are full of blood.' This was the reason why all their religiousness, and orthodoxy, and church-going, and praying, was only disgusting to God; because there was no righteousness with it. Their faith was only a dead, rotten, sham faith, for it brought forth no fruits of justice and love; and their religion was only hypocrisy, for it did not make them holy. No doubt they thought themselves pious and sincere enough; no doubt they thought that they were pleasing God perfectly, and giving Him all that He could fairly ask of them; no doubt they were fiercely offended at Isaiah's message to them; no doubt they could not understand what he meant by calling them a hypocritical nation, a second Sodom and Gomorrah, while they were destroying idols, and keeping the law of Moses, and worshipping God more earnestly than He had been worshipped since Solomon's time. But so it was. That was the message of God to them; that was the vision of Isaiah concerning them; that there was no soundness in the whole of the nation, 'from the sole of the foot to the crown of the head, nothing but wounds, and bruises, and putrefying sores,'—that is, that their whole heart and conscience, and ways of thinking, were utterly rotten, and abominable in the sight of God, even while they were holding the true doctrines about them, 'and keeping up the pure worship of Him. This, says the Lord, is not the way to please me. 'He hath showed thee, oh man, what is good. And what doth the Lord require of thee, but to do justly, and to love mercy, and to walk humbly with thy God?' To do justly, to love mercy, and then to walk humbly, sure that when you seem to have done all your duty, you have left only too much of it undone; even as St. Paul felt when he said, that though he knew nothing against himself; though he could not recollect a single thing in which he had failed of his duty to the Corinthians, yet that did not justify him. 'For he that judgeth me,' he says, 'is the Lord.' He sees deeper than I can; and He, alas! may take a very different view of my conduct from what I do; and this life of mine, which looks to me, from my ignorance, so spotless and perfect, may be, in His eyes, full of sins, and weakness, and neglects, and shameful follies. 'To walk humbly with God.' Not to believe that because you read the Bible, and have heard the gospel, and are sharp at finding out false doctrine in preachers, and belong to the Church of England, that therefore you know all about God, and can look down upon poor papists, and heathens, and say, 'This people, which knoweth not the law, is accursed: but *we* are enlightened, we understand the whole Bible, we know everything about God's will, and man's duty; and whosoever differs from us, or pretends to teach us anything new about God, must be wrong.' Not to do so, my friends, but to believe what St. Paul tells us solemnly; 'That if any man think that he knows anything, he knows nothing yet as he ought to know'—to believe that the Great God, and the will of God, and the love of God, and the mystery of Redemption, and the treasures of wisdom which are in His Bible, are, as St. Paul told you, boundless, like a living well, which can never be fathomed, or drawn dry, but fills again with fresh water as fast as you draw from it. That is walking humbly with God; and those who do not do so, but like the Pharisees of old, believe that they have all knowledge, and can understand all the mysteries of the Bible, and go through the world, despising and cursing all parties but their own—let them beware, lest the Lord be saying of them, as He said of the church of Sardis, of old, 'Thou sayest, I am rich, and increased with goods, and have need of nothing, and knowest not that thou art wretched, and miserable, and poor, and blind, and naked.'

How is this? What is this strange thing, without which even the true knowledge of doctrine is of no use; which, if a man, or a nation has not, he is poor, and blind, and wretched, and naked in soul, in spite of all his religion? Isaiah will tell us —What did he say to the Jews in his day?—

'Wash you, make you clean; put away the evil of your doings from before my eyes. Do justice to the fatherless, and relieve the widow!' 'Do that,' says the Lord, 'and then your repentance will be sincere. Church building, and church going are well—but they are not repentance,—churches are not souls. I ask you for your hearts, and you give me fine stones and fine words. I want souls—

I want *your* souls—I want you to turn to me. And what am I? saith the Lord. I am justice, I am love, I am the God of the oppressed, the fatherless, the widow.—That is my character. Turn to justice, turn to love, turn to mercy; long to be made just, and loving, and merciful; see that your sin has been just this, and nothing else, that you have been unjust, unloving, unmerciful. Repent for your neglect and cruelty, and repent in dust and ashes, when you see what wretched hypocrites you really are. And then, my boundless mercy and pardon shall be open to you. As you wish to be to me, so will I be to you; if you wish to become merciful, you shall taste my mercy; if you wish to become loving to others, you shall find that I love you; if you wish to become just, you shall find that I am just, just to deal by you as you deal by others; faithful and just to forgive you your sins, and to cleanse you from all unrighteousness. And then, all shall be forgiven and forgotten; 'though your sins be as scarlet, they shall be white as snow: though they be red like crimson, they shall be as wool.'

Surely, my friends, these things are worth taking to heart; for this is the sin which most destroys all men and nations—High religious profession with an ungodly, covetous, and selfish life. It is the worst and most dangerous of all sins; for it is like a disease which eats out the heart and life without giving pain; so that the sick man never suspects that anything is the matter with him, till he finds himself, to his astonishment, at the point of death. So it was with the Jews, three times in their history. In the time of Isaiah, under King Hezekiah; in the time of Jeremiah, under King Josiah; and last and worst of all, in the time of Jesus Christ. At each of these three times the Jews were high religious professors, and yet at each of these three times, they were abominable before God, and on the brink of ruin. In Isaiah's time their eyes seemed to have been opened at last to their own sins. Their fearful danger, and wonderful deliverance from the Assyrians, of which you heard last Sunday, seem to have done that for them; as God intended it should. During the latter part of Hezekiah's reign they seemed to have turned to God with their hearts, and not with their lips only; and Isaiah can find no words to express the delight which the blessed change gives him. Nevertheless, they soon fell back again into idolatry; and then there was another outward lip-reformation under the good king Josiah; and Jeremiah had to give them exactly the same warning which Isaiah had given them nearly a hundred years before. But that time, alas! they would not take the warning; and then all the evil which had been prophesied against them came on them. From hypocritical profession, they fell back again into their old idolatry; their covetousness, selfishness, party quarrels, and profligate lives made them too weak and rotten to stand against Nebuchadnezzar, king of Babylon, when he attacked them; and Jerusalem was miserably destroyed, the temple burnt, and the Jews carried captives to Babylon. There they repented in bitter sorrow and slavery; and God allowed them after seventy years to return to their own land. Then at first they seemed to be a really converted people, and to be worshipping God in spirit and in truth. They never again fell back into the idolatry of the heathen. So far from it; they became the greatest possible haters of it; they went on keeping the law of God with the utmost possible strictness, even to the day when the Lord Jesus appeared among them. Their religious people, the Scribes and Pharisees, were the most strict, moral, devout people of the whole world. They worshipped the very words and letters of the Bible; their thoughts seemed filled with nothing but God and the service of God: and yet the Lord Jesus told them that they were in a worse state, greater sinners in the sight of God, than they had ever been; that they, who hated idolatry, were filling up the measure of their idolatrous forefathers' iniquity; that the guilt of all the righteous blood shed on earth was to fall on them; that they were a race of serpents, a generation of vipers; and that even He did not see how they could escape the damnation of hell. And they proved how true His words were, by crucifying the very Lord of whom their much-prized Scriptures bore witness, whom they pretended to worship day and night continually; and received the just reward of their deeds in forty years of sedition, bloodshed, and misery, which ended by the Romans coming and sweeping the nation of the Jews from off the face of the earth.

So much for profession without practice. So much for true doctrine with dishonest and unholy lives. So much for outward respectability with inward sinfulness. So much for hating idolatry, while all the while men's hearts are far from God!

Oh! my friends, let us all search our hearts carefully in these times of high profession and low practice; lest we be adding our drop of hypocrisy to the great flood of it which now stifles this land of England, and so fall into the same condemnation as the Jews of old, in spite of far nobler examples, brighter and wider light, and more wonderful and bounteous blessings.

XXI.
THE UNFAITHFUL SERVANT.

LUKE xii. 45, 46.

But and if that servant say in his heart, My lord delayeth his coming; and shall begin to beat the men servants and the maid servants, and to eat and drink and to be drunken; the lord of that servant will come in a day when he looketh not for him, and in an hour when he is not aware, and will cut him asunder, and will appoint him his portion with the unbelievers.

BUT why with the unbelievers? The man had not disbelieved that he had any Lord at all; he had only believed that his Lord delayed his coming. And why was he to be put with those who do not believe in him at all? This is a very fearful question, friends, for us, when we think how it is the fashion among us now, to believe that our Lord delays His coming.—And surely most of us do believe that? For is it not our notion that, when the Lord Jesus ascended up to heaven, He went away a great distance off, perhaps millions of miles beyond the stars; and that He will not come back again till the last day—which, for aught we know, and as we rather expect, may not happen for hundreds or thousands of years to come? Is not that most people's notion, rich as well as poor ? And if that is not believing that our Lord delays His coming, what is?

But, you may answer, the Creed says plainly, that He ascended into heaven and sits at the right hand of God. Ah! my friends, those great words of the Creed which you take into your lips every Sunday, mean the very opposite to what most people fancy. They do not say, 'The Lord Jesus has left this poor earth to itself and its misery:' but they say, 'Lo, He is with you, even to the end of the world.' True, He is ascended into heaven. And how far off is heaven?—for so far off is the Lord Jesus, and no further. Not so far off, my friends, after all, if you knew where to find it. Truly said the great and good poet, now gone home to his reward—

> Heaven lies about us in our infancy.

And if we lose sight of it as we grow up to be men and women, it is not because heaven goes further off, but because we grow less heavenly. Even now, so close is heaven to us, that any one of us might enter into heaven this moment, without stirring from his seat. One real cry from the depths of your heart—'Father, forgive thy sinful child!'—one real feeling of your own worthlessness, and weakness, and emptiness, and of God's righteousness, and love, and mercy, ready for you

THE UNFAITHFUL SERVANT.

—and you are in heaven there and then, as near the feet of the blessed Lord Jesus, as Mary Magdalen was, when she tried to clasp them in the garden. I am serious, my friends; I am not given to talk fine figures of poetry; I am talking sober, straightforward, literal truth. And the Lord sits at God's right hand too? you believe that? Then how far off is God?—for as far off as God is, so far off is the Lord Jesus, and no further. What says St. Paul? That 'God is not far off from any one of us—for in Him we live, and move, and have our being' . . . IN Him . . . How far off is that? And is not God everywhere, if indeed we can say that He is anywhere? Then the Lord Jesus, who is at God's right hand, is everywhere also—here, now, with us this day. One would have thought that there was no need to prove that by argument, considering that His own blessed lips told us, 'Lo, I am with you, even to the end of the world;' and again, 'Wheresoever two or three are gathered together in my name, there am I in the midst of them.' And this is the Lord whom people fancy is gone away far above the stars, till the end of time! Oh, my friends, rather bow your heads before Him here this moment. For here He is among us now, listening to every thought of our poor sinful hearts. . . . . He is where God is—God *in* whom we live, and move, and have our being—and that is everywhere. Do you wish Him to be any nearer, my friends? Or do you—do you—take care what your hearts answer, for He is watching them—do you in the depth of your hearts wish that He were a little further off? Does the notion of His being here on this earth, watching and interfering (as we call it now-a-days in our atheism) with us and everything, seem unpleasant and burdensome? Is it more comfortable to you to think that He is away far up beyond the stars? Do you feel the lighter and freer for fancying that He will not visit the earth for many a year to come? In short, is it in your *hearts* that you are saying, The Lord delays His coming?

That is a very important question. For mind, a pious man might be, as many a pious man has been in these days, deceived by bad teaching into the notion that Jesus Christ was gone far away. But if he were a truly pious man, if he truly loved the Lord, that would be a painful thought—as I should have fancied, an unbearable thought—to him, when he looked out upon this poor miserable, confused world. He would be crying night and day, 'Oh, that thou wouldest rend the heavens and come down!' He would be in an agony of pity for this poor deserted earth, and of longing for the Saviour of it to come back and save it. He would never have a moment's peace of mind till he had

THE UNFAITHFUL SERVANT. 283

either seen the Lord come back again in His glory, or till he had found out—what I am sure the blessed Lord would teach him as a reward for his love—that it was all a dream and a nightmare, and that the Lord of the earth was in the earth, and close to him, all along; only that his weak eyes were held so that he did not know the Lord and the Lord's works when he saw them.

But that was not the temper of this servant in the Lord's parable. I am afraid it is by no means the temper of many of us now-a-days. The servant said *in his heart*, that his master would be long away. It was his heart put the thought into his head. He took to the notion *heartily*, as we say, because he was glad to believe it was true; glad to think that his master would not come to 'interfere' with him; and that in the meantime he might be lord and master himself, and treat every one in the house as if he himself, was the owner of it, and tyrannize over his fellow-servants, and enjoy himself in luxury and good living. So says David of the fool, 'The fool hath said in his heart, there is no God;' his heart puts that thought into his head. He wishes to believe that there is no God; and when there is a will there is a way; and he soon finds out reasons and arguments enough to prove what he is so very anxious to prove.

Now, my friends, I am afraid that there is not so much difference as people fancy, between the fool who says in his heart, 'There is no God,' and the fool who says in his heart, 'My Master delays His coming.'—'God has left the world to us and we must shift for ourselves in it.' The man who likes to be what St. Paul calls 'without God in the world,' is he so very much wiser than the man who likes to have no God at all? St. James did not think so; for what does he say— 'Thou believest that there is one God? Thou doest well—the devils also believe and tremble.' They know as much as that; but it does them no good—only increases their fear. 'But wilt thou know, oh! vain man, that faith without works,' believing without doing, 'is dead?' And are not too many, as I said just now, afraid of the thought of God; so afraid of it that they wish to allow the Son of God as little share as possible in the management of this world? Have not too many a belief without works; a mere belief that there is one God and not two, which hardly, from one year's end to another, makes them do one single thing which they would not have done if they had believed that there was no God at all? Fear of the law; fear of the policeman; fear of losing their work or their custom; fear of losing their neighbour's good word—that is what keeps most people from breaking loose. There is not much of the fear of God in that, or the love of God either, as far as I can see. They go through life as if they had made a covenant with God, that He should have his own way in the world to come, if He would only let them have their way in this world. Oh! my friends, my friends, do you think God is God of the next world and not of this world also? Do you think the kingdom, and the power, and the glory will be His a great many hundreds of years hence, in what you call heaven; and will not see what every page of Scripture tells you, what you yourself say every time you repeat the Lord's Prayer, that the Kingdom, and the Power, and the Glory are His now, here, in this life, and that He has committed all things to His Son Jesus Christ and given the power into His hand, that He may rule this earth in righteousness now, here, in this life, and conquer back for God one by one, if it be possible, every creature upon earth? So says the Bible—and people profess now-a-days to believe their Bibles. My friends, too many, now-a-days, while they profess very loudly to believe what the Bible says, only believe what their favourite teachers tell them that the Bible says. If they really read their Bibles for themselves, and took God at His word, there would be less tyrannizing of one man over another, less grinding down

of men by masters, and of men by each other—
for the poor are often very hard on each other in
England, now, my friends—very envious and
spiteful, and slanderous about each other. They
say that dog wont eat dog—yet how many a
poor man grudges and supplants his neighbour,
and tries to get into his place and beat him
down in his wages. And there are those who
call themselves learned men, who tell the poor
that that is God's will, and the way by which
God intends them to prosper. If those men
believed their Bibles, they would be repenting in
sackcloth and ashes for having preached such a
devil's sermon to God's children. If men really
read their Bibles, there would be less eating and
drinking with the drunken; less idleness and
luxury among the rich; less fancying that a man
has a right to do what he likes with his own,
because all men would know that they were only
the Lord's stewards, bound to give an account to
Him of the good which they had done with what
He has lent them. There would be fewer parents
fancying that they can tyrannize over their children,
bringing them up as heathens for the sake of the
few pence they earn; using bad language, and
doing shameful things before them, which they
dared not do if they recollected that the Lord was
looking on; beating and scolding them as if they
were brutes or slaves, to save themselves the

trouble of teaching them gently what the poor little creatures cannot know without being taught : and most shameful of all, robbing the poor children of their little earnings to spend it themselves in drunkenness. Ah, blessed Lord! if people did but know how near Thou wert to them, all that would vanish out of England, as the night clouds vanish away before the sun !

And He is near, my friends: He is watching; He is governing ; He is at hand : and in this life or in the life to come, forget Him as we choose, He will make us know plain enough, and without any doubt whatsoever, that He is the Lord.

He has fulfilled this awful parable of His about the unfaithful servant already; many a time, against many a man, many a great king, and prince, and nation ; and He will fulfil it against each and every man, from the nobleman in his castle to the labourer in his cottage, who says in his heart, 'My Lord delays his coming,' and begins to tyrannize over those who are weaker than himself, and to enjoy himself as he likes, and forget that he is not his own, but bought with the price of Christ's blood, and bound to work for Christ's kingdom and glory.

So He punished the popes of Rome, three hundred years ago. When all the nations in Europe were listening to them and obeying them, and they had put into their hands by God a greater power of doing good than He ever gave to any human being before or since, what did they do? Instead of using their power for Christ, they used it for themselves. Instead of preaching to all nations the good news that Christ the Son of God was their King, they said, ' I, the pope, am your king. Christ is gone far away into heaven, and has committed all power on earth to us; we are Christ's vicars; we are in Christ's place; He has entrusted to our keeping all the treasures of His merits and His grace, and no one can get any blessing from Christ, unless we choose to give it him.' So they said in their hearts just what the foolish servant in the parable said: and fancying that they were lords and masters, naturally enough went on to behave as such; to beat the menservants and maid-servants, that is, to oppress and tyrannize over the bodies and minds and consciences of men, and women too, God knows; and to eat and drink with the drunken, to live in riot and debauchery. But the Lord was not so far off as those foolish popes fancied. And in an hour when they were not aware, He came and cut them asunder. He snatched from them one half of the nations of Europe, and England among the rest; He punished them by doubt, ignorance, confusion, and utter blindness, and appointed them their portion among the unbelievers in such terrible earnest, that to this very day, to judge by the things which they say and do, it is difficult to persuade ourselves that the popes really believe in any God at all.

So He did, only three years ago, to many kings and princes on the continent.* They professed to be Christians; but they had forgotten that they were Christ's stewards, that all their power came from Him, and that He had given it them only to use for the good of their subjects. And they too went on saying—'The Lord delays His coming, we are rulers in this world, and God is ruler in the world to come.' So they, too, oppressed their subjects, and lived in ease on what they wrung out of the poor wretches below them. But the Lord was nearer them, too, than they fancied; and all at once—as they were fancying themselves all safe and prosperous, and saying, 'We are those who ought to speak, who is Lord over us?'—their fool's paradise crumbled from under their feet. A few paltry mobs of foolish starving people, without weapons, without leaders, without good counsel to guide them, rose against them. And what did they do? They might have crushed down the rebels most of them, in a week, if they had had courage. And in the only country where the rebels were really strong, that is in Austria,

* In 1848-9.

all might have been quiet again at once, if the king had only had the heart to do common justice, and keep his own solemn oaths. But no—the terror of the Lord came upon them. He most truly cut them in sunder. They were every man of a different mind, and none of them in the same mind a day together; they became utterly conscience-stricken, terrified, perplexed, at their wit's end, not having courage or determination to do anything, or even to do nothing, and fled shamefully away one after another, to their everlasting disgrace. And those of them who have got back their power since are showing sadly enough, by their obstinate folly and wickedness, that the Lord has appointed them their portion with the unbelievers, and left them to fill up the measure of their iniquity, and drink deep the cup of wrath which is in His hand, full and mixed for those who forget God.

Oh! my friends, let us lay these things solemnly to heart. Do not fancy that the Lord will punish the wicked great, and forget the wicked small. In His sight there is neither great nor small; all are small enough for Him to crush like the moth; and all are too great to be overlooked, or forgotten by Him, without whom not a sparrow falls to the ground. Again I say, my friends, let us lay His parable to heart. Let us who have property, and station, and education, never forget who has given it us, and for whom we must use it. Let us never forget that to whom much is given, of them will much be required. Let us pray to the Lord daily to write upon our inmost hearts those solemn words, 'Who made thee to differ from another; and what hast thou which thou didst not receive?' Let us look on our servants, our labourers, on every human being over whom we have any influence, as weaker brothers whom God has commanded us to help, teach, and guide in body, mind, and spirit, not that we may make them our slaves, but make them free, manful, self-helping, and in due time independent of us and of every one except God.

And you young people, who have no authority over any one, but over your own bodies; to whom the Lord has given little or nothing to manage and take care of except your own health and strength —do not let the devil tempt you to believe that that health and strength is your own property, to do what you like with. It belongs to the Lord who died for you, and He will require an account from you how you have used it. Do not let the devil tempt you to believe that the Lord delays his coming to you—that you may do what you like now, in the prime of your years, and that it will be time enough to think about God and religion when God visits you with cares, and sickness, and old age.

That is the fancy of too many; but it will surely turn out to be a mistake. Those who misuse their youth, and health, and strength, in tyrannizing over those who are weaker than themselves, and laughing at those who are not as clever as themselves, and eating and drinking with the drunken—the Lord will come to them in an hour when they are not aware, and cut them asunder, in some way or other, by loss of work, or poverty, or sickness, or doubt and confusion, and bitter shame and perplexity of mind ; till they find out, poor things, that they have been living like the unbelievers all their youth, without God in the world, while God's love and God's teaching, and God's happiness was ready for them ; and have to go back again to their Father and their Lord, and cry, ' Father, we have sinned against heaven and before Thee, and are no more worthy to be called Thy children !' Oh, you who have been fancying that the Lord was gone far away, and that you had a right to do what you liked with the powers which He has given you, go back to Him, now at once, and confess that you, and all belonging to you, belong to Him, and ask Him to teach you how to use it aright. Ask Him to teach you how to please Him with it, and not yourselves only. Ask Him to teach you how to do good to all around you, and not merely to do what you like. Ask Him to show you how to do your duty to Him, and to your neighbours, for whom He died on the cross, in that station of life to which He has called you. Ask Him to show you how to use your property, your knowledge, your business, your strength, your health, so that you may be a blessing and a help to those whom He blesses and helps, and who, He wishes, should bless and help each other. Go back to Him at once, my friends. You will not have far to go, seeing that He is now even among us here hearing my clumsy words; and I do hope, and trust, and pray, bringing them home to some of your hearts with that spirit and power of His, which is like a two-edged sword, piercing to the very depths of a man's heart, and showing him how ugly it is—and how noble the Lord will make it, if he will but repent, and pray to Him who never cast out any that came to Him.

XXII.

THE WAY TO WEALTH.

Isaiah lv. 6, 7.

Seek ye the Lord while He may be found, call ye upon Him while He is near: let the wicked forsake his way, and the unrighteous man his thoughts: and let him return unto the Lord, and He will have mercy upon him, and to our God, for He will abundantly pardon.

SOME of you, surely, while the first lesson was being read this morning, must have felt the beauty of it; and if you were thoughtful, perplexed, weary, sad at heart, perhaps you felt that it was more than beautiful—that it was full of comfort. And so it should be full of comfort to you, my friends. God meant it to give you comfort. For though it was written and spoken by a man of like passions with ourselves, it was just as truly written and spoken by God, who made heaven and earth. It is true and everlasting, the message which it brings, and like all true and everlasting words, it is the voice of God who cannot change; who makes no difference between Jew and Gentile, between us in England here, and nations which perished hundreds of years ago.

THE WAY TO WEALTH. 295

And what is its message? What was God's word to the old Jews, among all their sin, and sorrow, and labour?

Is it the message of a stern judge, saying 'Pay me that thou owest, to the uttermost farthing; and if you cannot do that, fret and torment yourselves in shame and terror here on earth, for all your sins, if, possibly, you may chance to change my mind, and find forgiveness at the last day?'

Is it the message of a proud tyrant, saying, 'If you are miserable, and fallen, and sinful, what is that to me? I am perfect, blest, contented with myself, alone in my glory, far away beyond the sight of men, beyond the sun and stars—what are you worms of earth to me?'

Or is it the voice of a loving Father, calling to his self-willed children who have gone proudly and boldly away from their Father's house, and thrown off their Father's government, and said in their conceit, 'We are men. Do not we know good and evil? Do we not know what is our interest? Cannot we judge for ourselves, and shift for ourselves, and take care of ourselves? Why are we to be barred from pleasant things here, and profitable things there? We will be our own masters.'

To self-willed children who have said thus, and done thus in their foolish hearts, and have found all their conceit, and shrewdness, only lead them into sorrow, and perplexity, and distress.—Who have found that with all their cleverness they could not get the very good things for which they left their Father's house ; or if they get them, find no enjoyment in them, but only discontent, and shame, and danger, and a sad self-accusing heart—spending their money for that which does not feed them after all, and labouring hard for things which do not satisfy them ; always longing for something more— always finding the pleasure, or the profit, or the honour which a little way off looked so fine, look quite ugly and worthless, when they come up to it and get hold of it—finding all things full of labour ; the eye never satisfied with seeing, or the ear with hearing ; the same thing coming over and over again. Each young man starting with gay hopes, as if he were the first man that ever was born, and he was going to do out of hand such fine things as man never did before, and make his own fortune, and set the world to right at once; and then as he grows older, falling into the same weary ruts as his forefathers went dragging on in, every fresh year bringing its own labour, and its own sorrow ; and dying like them, taking nothing away with him of all he has earned, and crying with his last breath, 'That which is crooked cannot be made straight, and that which is wanting cannot be numbered. What profit hath a man of all his labour which he taketh under the sun, for all is vanity and vexation of spirit?'—

To self-willed children, who have tried their own way ever since they were born, they and their fathers before them, and found it go round in a ring and leave them just where they started in heart and soul, and, on their death-beds, in purse and power also—

To such struggling, dissatisfied beings—such as nine-tenths of the men and women on this earth, alas! are still—comes the word of this loving Father—

'Ho, every one that thirsteth, come ye to the waters! and he that hath no money, come, buy and eat. Yea, come, buy wine and milk without money, and without price.' Why do you fancy that money can give you all you want? Why this labouring and straining after money, as if it was God, as if it made heaven and earth, and all therein? Is money a God? or money's worth? 'I am God,' saith the Lord, 'and beside me there is none else. It is I who give, and not money. It is I who save men, and not money. And I do save, and I do give freely to all. Come, and try my mercy, and see if my word be not true.' This struggling and snarling, like dogs over a bone—what profit comes of it? are you happier? are you wiser? are you better? are you more at peace with your neighbours; more at peace with your own hearts and consciences? If you are, money has not made you so, nor plotting, and scraping, and struggling, and pushing your neighbour down, that you may rise a few inches on his shoulders. No. Hear what the voice of your Father says is the true way to wealth and comfort, after which you all struggle and labour so hard in vain.—' Hearken diligently unto me, and you shall eat that which is good, and your soul shall delight itself in fatness. Incline your ear and come unto me. Hear, and your soul shall live. And I will make an everlasting covenant with you, even the sure mercies,' or rather 'the faithful oath which I sware unto David.' And what is this faithful oath which God sware to David.—'Of the fruit of thy body, I will set on thy seat?' A promise of a righteous king who should arise in David's family. How far David understood the full meaning of that glorious promise we cannot tell. He thought most probably, at first, that Solomon, his son, was to be the king who would fulfil it. But all through many of his psalms, there are deep and great words about some nobler and more perfect king than Solomon—about one who, as Isaiah says here, would perfectly witness to the people that God was their King; one who would be a perfect leader and commander of the people; a holy one of Israel, who would sit on God's right hand; to hear the good news of whom, the Jews would call nations whom they then did not know of, and for whose sake nations who did not know them would run to them. And dimly David did see this, that God would raise up a true Christ, that is, one truly anointed by God, chosen and sent out by God, to sit on his throne, and be perfectly what David was only in part; a King made perfect by suffering, a King of poor men, a King who bore the sins and carried the iniquities of all His people, from the highest to the lowest. We know who that was. We know clearly what David only knew dimly, what Isaiah only knew a little more clearly. We know who was born of the Virgin Mary, crucified under Pontius Pilate, ascended into heaven, and now sits at the right hand of God, ever praying for us, ruling the world in righteousness, Jesus the Lord, the Holy One of Israel, to whom all power is given in heaven and earth.

But Isaiah, though he knew Him only dimly, still knew Him. He did not know that the Lord, the Holy One of Israel, would take on Himself the form of a poor man, and be called the son of the carpenter. Such boundless love and condescension in the Son of God he never could have fancied for himself, and God had not chosen to reveal it to him; or to any one else in those days. But this he did see, that the Lord Jesus, He whom he calls the Holy One of Israel, was near the Jews in his time; that He was watching over them, mourning over their sins, arguing with them, and calling to them to return to Him with most human love and tenderness, as a husband to the woman whom he loves in spite of her unfaithfulness to him. As he says to his sinful and distressed country in the chapter before this—'Thy Maker is thy husband: the Lord of Hosts is His name, and thy Redeemer is the Holy One of Israel, the Lord of the whole earth shall He be called. For the Lord hath called thee as a woman forsaken and grieved in spirit. For a small moment have I forsaken thee, but with great mercies will I gather thee. In a little anger I hid my face from thee for a moment, but with everlasting kindness will I have mercy on thee, saith the Lord thy Redeemer.'

This, then, Isaiah knew—that the heart of the Holy Lord pitied and yearned after those poor sinful Jews, as a husband's after a foolish and sinful wife. And how much more should we believe the same, how much more should we believe that His heart pities and yearns for all foolish and sinful people here in England now! We who know a thousand times more than Isaiah knew of His love, His pity, His condescension, which led Him to sacrifice Himself upon the cross for us? Surely, surely, if Isaiah had a right to say to those Jews 'Seek the Lord while He may be found,' I have a thousand times as much right to say it to you. If Isaiah had a right to say to those Jews, 'Let the wicked forsake his ways, and the unrighteous man his thoughts, and let him return unto the Lord, and He will have mercy upon him, and to our God, for He will abundantly pardon,' then I have a right to say it to you.

Free mercy, utter pardon, pardon for all, even for the worst. And what is the argument which Isaiah uses to make his countrymen repent? Is it 'Repent, or you shall be damned : Repent because God's wrath and curse is against you? The Lord hates you and despises you, and you must crawl to His feet, like beaten hounds, and intreat Him not to strike you into hell as He intends?' Not so; it was because God loved the Jews, that they were to repent. It is because God loves you that you must repent, 'Incline your ear,' saith the Lord, 'and come unto me, hear, and your soul shall live; and you shall eat that which is good, and your soul shall delight itself in fatness.' Yes, God is love. God's delight and glory is to give; in spite of all our sins He gives and gives, sending rain and fruitful seasons to just and unjust, to fill their hearts with joy and gladness; and all the while men fancy that it is not God that gives, but they who take. God has not left Himself, as St. Paul says, without a witness; every fruitful shower and quickening gleam of sunshine cries to us—See! God is love: He is the giver. And men will not hear that voice. They say in their hearts, 'The Lord is far away above the skies; He does not care for us: we must help ourselves, each man to what he can get off this earth; nay even when we are hard put to it for a living, we must break God's laws to keep ourselves alive, and so steal from God's table the very good things which he offers us freely.'

But some will say, 'He does not give freely: we must work and struggle. Why do you mock poor hard-worked creatures with such words as these?'

Ask that question of God, my friends, and not of me. Isaiah said that those who hearkened to God diligently should eat what is good. The Lord Jesus Christ Himself said the same—that if we seek first the kingdom of God and His justice, all other things should be added to them. He did not mean us to be idle, God forbid! but this He meant, that if we, each in his business and calling, put steadily before ourselves what is right, what God would wish us, His subjects, to be in His kingdom—if instead of making our first thought in every business we take in hand, 'What will suit my interest best, what will raise most money, what will give me most pleasure?" we said to ourselves all day long, 'What will be most right, and just, and merciful for us to do; what will be most pleasing to a God who is love and justice itself? what will do most good to my neighbour as well as myself?' then all things would go well with us. Then we should be prosperous and joyful. Then our plans would succeed and our labour bring forth real profit to us, because they would be according to the will of God: we should be fellow-workers with Jesus Christ in the great work of doing good to this poor distracted world, and His help and blessing would be with us.

And if you ask me, how can this come to pass? I must answer, as Isaiah does in this same chapter, 'The Lord's ways are not as our ways, nor His thoughts as our thoughts, but higher than ours, as the heavens are above the earth.' But if we do turn to God, and repent each man of us of his selfishness, his unfaithfulness, his hard-heartedness, his covetousness, his self-will, his ungodliness—then God's blessing, as Isaiah says, will come down on us, and spring up among us, we know not how or whence, like the rain and snow, which comes down from heaven and waters the earth, and makes it bud and bring forth to give seed to the sower and bread to the eater. So shall be the Lord's word, which goes out of His mouth; it will not return to Him void, but will accomplish what He pleases, and prosper in that whereto he sends it. He will teach us and guide us in the right way. He will put His word into the mouths of true teachers to show us our duty. He will pour out His spirit upon us, to make us love our duty. In one way and another, we know not how, we shall be taught what is good for England, good for each parish, good for each family. And wealth, peace, and prosperity for rich and poor will be the fruit of obeying the word of God, and giving up our hearts to be led by His spirit. As it was to be in Judæa of old, if they repented, so will it be with us. They should go forth with joy and do their work in peace. The hills should break before them into singing, and all the trees of the field should clap their hands; instead of thorns should come up timber trees : instead of briers, garden shrubs. The whole cultivation of the country was to improve, and be to the Lord for a name, and a sign for ever that the true way to wealth and prosperity, is the way of God, justice, mercy to each other, and obedience to the will of Him who made heaven and earth, trees and fruitful fields, rain and sunshine, and gives the blessings of them freely to His children of mankind, in proportion as they look up to Him as a loving Father, and return to Him day by day, with childlike repentance, and full desire to amend their lives according to His holy word.

XXIII.

THE LOVE OF CHRIST.

2 COR. V. 14, 15.

For the love of Christ constraineth us; because we thus judge, that if one died for all, then were all dead. And that He died for all, that they which live should not henceforth live unto themselves, but unto Him which died for them, and rose again.

WHAT is the use of sermons?—what is the use of books? Here are hundreds and thousands of people hearing weekly and daily what is right, and how many *do* what is right?—much less *love* what is right? What can be the reason of this, that men should know the better and choose the worse? What motive can one find out?—what reason or argument can one put before people, to make them do their duty? How can one stir them up to conquer themselves; to conquer their own love of pleasure, laziness, cowardice, conceit, above all their own selfishness, and do simply what is right, morning, noon, and night? That is a question worth asking and considering, for there ought to be some use in sermons and in books; and there ought to be some use in every one of us too. Woe to the man who is of no use! The Lord have mercy on his soul; for he needs it! It is, indeed, worth his while to take any trouble which will teach him a motive for being useful; in plain words, stir him up to do his duty, to do his rights; for a man's rights are not, as the world thinks, what is right others should do to him, but what is right he should do to others. Our duty is our right, the only thing which is right for us. What motive will constrain us, that is, bind us, and force us to do that?

Will self-interest? Will a man do right because you tell him it is his interest, it will pay him to do it? Look round you and see.—The drunkard knows that drinking will ruin him, and yet he gets drunk. The spendthrift knows that extravagance will ruin him, and yet he throws away his money still. The idler knows that he is wasting his only chance for all eternity, and yet he puts the thought out of his head, and goes on idling. The cheat knows that he is in danger of being almost certainly found out sooner or later; he knows too that he is burdening his own conscience with the curse of inward shame and self-contempt; and yet he goes on cheating. The hard master knows, or ought to know (for there is quite enough to prove it to him) that it would pay him better in the long run to be more merciful, and less covetous; that by grinding those whom he employs down to the last farthing, he degrades them till they become burdens on him and curses to him; that what he gains by high prices, he will lose in the long run by bad debts; that what he saves in low wages, he will pay in extra poor-rates; and that even if he does make money out of the flesh and bones of those beneath him, that money ill gotten is sure to be ill spent, that there is a curse on it, that it brings a curse in the gnawing of a man's own conscience, and a curse too in the way it flows away from his family as fast as it flowed to them. 'He that by usury and unjust gain increases his wealth, shall gather for him that will pity the poor.' So said Solomon of old. And men who worship Mammon find it come true daily, and see that, taking all things together, a man's life does not consist in the abundance of the things which he possesses, and that those who make such haste to be rich, fall, as the apostle says, 'into temptation and a snare, and pierce themselves through with many sorrows.' Such a man sees his neighbours making money, and making themselves more unhappy, anxious, discontented by it; he sees, in short, that it is not his interest to do nothing but make money and save money: and yet in spite of that, he thinks of nothing else. Self-interest cannot keep him from that sin. I do not believe that self-interest ever kept any man from any *sin*, though it may keep him from many an imprudence. Self-interest may make many a man respectable, but whom did it ever make good? You may as well make house walls of paper, or take a rush for a walking-stick, as take self-interest to keep you upright, or even prudent. The first shake—and the rush bends, and the paper wall breaks, and a man's selfish prudence is blown to the winds. Let pleasure tempt him, or ambition, or the lust of making money by speculation; let him take a spite against any one; let him get into a passion; let his pride be hurt; and he will do the maddest things, which he knows to be entirely contrary to his own interest, just to gratify the fancy of the moment. Those who call themselves philosophers, and fancy that men's self-interest, if they can only feel it strong enough, would make all men just and merciful to each other, know as little of human nature as they do of God or the devil.

What *will* make a man do his duty? Will the hope of heaven? That depends very much upon what you mean by heaven. But what people commonly mean by going to heaven, is—not going to hell. They believe that they must go to either one place or the other. They would much sooner of course stay on earth for ever, because their treasure is here, and their heart too. But that cannot be, and as they have no wish to go to hell, they take up with heaven instead, by way of making the best of a bad matter.

I ask you, solemnly, my friends, each one of you, which would you sooner do—stay here on earth, or go to Heaven? You need not answer *me*. I am afraid many of you would not dare answer me as you really felt, because you would be ashamed of not liking to go to heaven. But answer God. Answer yourselves in the sight of God. When you keep yourselves back from doing a wrong thing, because you know it is wrong, is it for love of heaven, or for mere fear of being punished in hell? Some of you will answer boldly at once, 'For neither one nor the other; when we keep from wrong, it is because we hate and despise what is wrong: when we do right, it is because it is right and we ought to do it. We can't explain it, but there is something in us which tells us we ought to do right.' Very good, my friends, I shall have a word to say to you presently; but in the mean time there are some others who have been saying to themselves, ' Well, I know we do right because we are afraid of being punished if we do not do it, but what of that? at all events we get the right thing done, and leave the wrong thing undone, and what more do you want? Why torment us with disagreeable questions as to *why* we do it.'

Now, my friends, to make the matter simpler, I will take you at your words, for the sake of argument. Suppose you do avoid sin from the fear of hell, does that make what you do *right?* Does that make *you* right? Does that make your heart right? It is a great blessing to a man's neighbours, certainly, if he is kept from doing wrong any how—by the fear of hell, or fear of jail, or fear of shame, or fear of ghosts if you like, or any other cowardly and foolish motive—a great blessing to a man's neighbours: but no blessing, that I can see, to the man himself. He is just the same; his heart is not changed; his heart is no more right in the sight of God, or in the sight of any man of common sense either, than it would be if he did the wrong thing, which he loves and dare not do. You feel that yourselves about other people. You will say 'That man has a bad heart, for all his respectable outside. He would be a rogue if he dared, and therefore he *is* a rogue.' Just so I say, my friends, take care lest God should say of you, 'He would be a sinner if he dared, and therefore he is a sinner.'

How can the hope of heaven, or the fear of hell, make a man do right? The right thing, the true thing for a man, is to be loving, and do loving things; and can fear of hell do that, or hope of heaven either? Can a man make himself affectionate to his children because he fancies he shall be punished if he is not so and rewarded if he is so? Will the hope of heaven send men out to feed the hungry, to clothe the naked, visit the sick, preach the gospel to the poor?—The Papists say it will. I say it will not. I believe that even in those who do these things from hope of heaven and fear of hell, there is some holier, nobler, more spiritual motive, than such everlasting selfishness, such perfect hypocrisy, as to do loving works for others, for the sake of one's own self-love.

What feeling then is there left which will bind a man to do good, not once in a way, but always and habitually? to do good not only to himself but to all around him? I know but of one, my friends, and that is Love. There are many sides to love—admiration, reverence, gratitude, pity, affection—they are all different shapes of that one great spirit of love. Surely all of you have felt its power more or less; how wonderfully it can conquer a man's whole heart, change his whole conduct. For love of a woman; for pity to those in distress; for admiration for any one who is nobler and wiser than himself; for gratitude to one who has done him kindness; for loyalty to one to whom he feels he owes a service—a man will dare to do things, and suffer things, which no self-interest or fear in the world could have brought him to. Do you not know it yourselves? Is it not fondness for your wives and children, that will make you slave and stint yourselves of pleasure more than any hope of gain could ever do? But there is no one human being, my friends, whom we can meet among us now, for whom we can feel all these different sorts of love? Surely not: and yet there must be One Person somewhere for whom God intends us to feel them all at once; or else He would not have given all these powers to us, and made them all different branches of one great root of love. There must be One Person somewhere, who can call out the whole love in us— all our gratitude; all our pity; all our admiration; all our loyalty; all our brotherly affection. *And there is One,* my friends. One who has done for us more than ever husband or father, wife or brother, can do to call out our gratitude. One who has suffered for us more than the saddest wretch upon this earth can suffer, to call out our pity. One who who is nobler, purer, more lovely in character, than all others who ever trod this earth, to call out our admiration. One who is wiser, mightier than all rulers and philosophers, to call out all our reverence. One who is tenderer, more gentle, more feeling-hearted, than the kindest woman who ever sat by a sick bed, to call out all our love. Of whom can I be speaking? Of whom but of Jesus; He who for us stooped

THE LOVE OF CHRIST.

out of the heaven of heavens; for us left His eternal glory in the bosom of the Father; for us took upon Him the form of a servant, and was born of a village maiden, and was called the son of a carpenter; for us wandered this earth for thirty years in sorrow and shame; for us gave His back to the scourge, and His face to shameful spitting; for us hung upon the cross, and died the death of the felon and the slave. Oh! my friends, if that story will not call out our love, what will? If we cannot admire Christ, whom can we admire? If we cannot be grateful to Christ, to whom can we be grateful? If we cannot pity Christ, whom can we pity? If we cannot feel bound in honour to live for Christ, to work for Christ, to delight in talking of Christ, thinking of Christ, to glory in doing Christ's commandments to the very smallest point, to feel no sacrifice too great, no trouble too petty, if we can please Christ by it and help forward Christ's kingdom upon earth—if we cannot feel bound in honour to do that for Christ, what honour is there in us? Again, I say, if we cannot love Christ, whom can we love? If the remembrance of what He has worked for us will not stir us up to work for Him, what will stir us up?

I say it again, we are bound by every tie, by every feeling that can bind man to man, to devote ourselves to Christ, the Man of all men. I say this is no dream or fancy, it is an actual fact, which thousands, and hundreds of thousands on this earth have felt. Nothing but love to Christ, nothing but loving Him because He first loved us, can constrain and force a man as with a mighty feeling which he cannot resist, to labour day and night for Christ's sake, and therefore for the sake of God the Father of Christ. What else do you suppose it was, which could have stirred up the apostles,— above all, that wise, learned, high-born, prosperous man St. Paul, to leave house and home, and wander in daily danger of his life? What does St. Paul say himself? 'The love of Christ constraineth us, because we thus judge, that if one died for all, then were all dead, and that He died for all, that they which live should not henceforth live unto themselves, but unto Him who died for them.' And what else could have kept St. Paul through all that labour and sorrow of his own choosing, of which he speaks in the chapter before?—' We are troubled on every side, yet not distressed; we are perplexed, but not in despair; persecuted, but not forsaken; cast down, but not destroyed; always bearing about in the body the dying of the Lord Jesus, that the life also of Jesus might be made manifest in our body; for we which live are alway delivered unto death for Jesus' sake, that the life also of Jesus might be made manifest in our body.'

We may say that St. Paul was an exceedingly benevolent man, and *that* made him do it; or that he had found out certain new truths and opinions which delighted him very much, and therefore he did it. But St. Paul gives no such account of himself: and we have no right to take any one's account but his own. He knew his own heart best. He does not say that he came to preach a scheme of redemption, or opinions about Christ. He says he came to preach nothing but Christ Himself— Christ crucified—to tell people about the Lord he loved, about the Lord who loved him, certain that when they had heard the plain story of Him, their hearts, if they were simple, and true, and loving, would leap up in answer to his words, and find out as by instinct, what Christ had done for them, what they were to do for Christ. Ay, I believe, my friends—indeed I am certain—from my own reading, that in every age and country, just in proportion as men have loved Christ personally as a man would love another man, just in that proportion have they loved their neighbours, worked for their neighbours, sacrificed their time, their pleasure, their money, to do good to all, for the sake of Him who commanded, 'If ye love *ME*, keep my commandments; and my commandment is this, that ye should love one another as I have loved you.' That is the only sure motive. All other motives for doing good or being good, will fail in one case or another case, because they do not take possession of a man's whole heart, but only of some part of his heart. Love—love to Christ, can alone sweep away a man's whole heart and soul with it, and renew it, and transfigure it, and make it strong instead of weak, pure instead of foul, gentle instead of fierce, brave instead of being vain and cowardly, and fearing what every one will say of him. Only love for Christ, who loved all men unto the death, will make us love all men too: not only one here and there who may agree with us or help us; but those who hate us, those who misunderstand us, those who thwart us, ay, even those who disobey and slight not only us, but Jesus Christ Himself. *That* is the hardest lesson of all to learn: but thousands have learnt it; every one ought to learn it. In proportion as a man loves Christ, he will learn to love those who do not love Christ. For Christ loves them whether they know it or not; Christ died for them whether they believe it or not; and we must love them because our Saviour loves them.

Oh! my friends, why do so few love Christ? Why do so few live as those who are not their own, but bought with the price of His precious blood and bound to devote themselves, body and soul, to His cause? Why do so many struggle against their sins, while yet they cannot break off those sins, but go struggling and sinning on, hating their sins and yet unable to break through their sins, like birds beating themselves to death against the wires of their cage? Why? Because they do not know Christ. And how can they know Him, unless they read their Bibles with simple, child-like hearts, determined to let the Bible tell its own story: believing that those who walked with Christ on earth, must know best what He was like? Why? Because they will not ask Christ to come and show Himself to them, and make them see Him, and love Him, and admire Him, whether they will or not. Oh! remember, if Christ be the Son of God, the Lord of heaven and earth, we cannot go to Him, poor, weak, ignorant creatures as we are. We cannot ascend up into heaven to bring Christ down. He must come down, out of His own great love and condescension, and dwell in our hearts as He has promised to do, if we do but love Him. He must come down and show Himself to us. Oh! read your Bibles—read the story of Christ, and if that does not stir up in you some love for Him, you must have hearts of stone, not flesh and blood. And then go to Him; pray to Him, whether you believe in Him altogether or not, upon the mere chance of His being able to hear you and help you. You would not throw away a chance on earth; will you throw away such a chance in heaven as having the Son of God to help you? Oh, cry to Him; say out of the depths of your heart, 'Thou most blessed and glorious Being who ever walked this earth, who hast gone blameless through all sorrow and temptation that man can feel; if Thou dost love any one, if Thou canst hear any one, hear me! If thou canst not help me, no one can. I have a hundred puzzling questions which I cannot answer for myself, a hundred temptations which I cannot conquer for myself, a hundred bad habits which I cannot shake off of myself; and they tell me that Thou canst teach me, Thou canst guide me, Thou canst strengthen me, Thou canst take out of my heart this shame and gnawing of an evil conscience. If Thou be the Son of God, make me clean! If it be true that Thou lovest all men, show Thy love to me! If it be true that Thou canst teach all men, teach me! If it be true that Thou canst help all men, help my unbelief, for if Thou dost not, there is no help for me in heaven or earth!' You, who are sinful, distracted, puzzled, broken-hearted, cry to Christ in that way, if you have no better way, and see if He does not hear you. He is not one to break the bruised reed, or quench the smoking flax. He will hear you, for He has heard all who have ever called on Him. Cry to

THE LOVE OF CHRIST. 319

Him from the bottom of your hearts. Tell Him that you do *not* love Him, and that yet you *long* to love Him. And see if you do not find it true that those who come to Christ, He will in no wise cast out. He may not seem to answer you the first time, or the tenth time, or for years; for Christ has His own deep, loving, wise ways of teaching each man, and for each man a different way. But try to learn all you can of Him. Try to know Him. Pray to know, and understand Him, and love Him. And sooner or later you will find His words come true, ' If a man love me, I and my Father will come to him, and take up our abode with him.' And then you will feel arise in you a hungering and a thirsting after righteousness, a spirit of love, and a desire of doing good, which will carry you up and on, above all that man can say or do against you—above all the laziness, and wilfulness, and selfishness, and cowardice which dwells in the heart of every one. You will be able to trample it all under foot for the sake ot being good and doing good, in the strength of that one glorious thought, ' Christ lived and died for me, and, so help me God, I will live and die for Christ.'

THE END.

www.ingramcontent.com/pod-product-compliance
Lightning Source LLC
Chambersburg PA
CBHW030738230426
43667CB00007B/759